teen poets

RAISED VOICES

Edited by Kelly Oliver

First published in Great Britain in 2003 by
YOUNG WRITERS
Remus House,
Coltsfoot Drive,
Peterborough, PE2 9JX
Telephone (01733) 890066

HB ISBN 1 84460 924 3
SB ISBN 1 84460 925 1

FOREWORD

As part of our ongoing pursuit to present a showcase of today's best up-and-coming authors, Young Writers is now proud to present its 'Teen Poets' series.

Few periods in life are more turbulent - or more crucial in human development than in the early teens. The struggles and trials faced daily can shape and mould our developing persona as we take a tentative step towards our early adult lives. The 'Teen Poets' series aims to bring these growing tribulations to light, providing a valuable snapshot into the thoughts and poetic visions of the teenage mind.

Raised Voices offers a selection of these poems, as the young writers within tackle a range of vital issues whilst also sharing with us the lighter side of teenage life. The result is a valuable and stimulating insight into the mind-set of the modern youth, and a challenging read for many years to come.

CONTENTS

The Poems

WE ARE ALL THE SAME INSIDE

Racism is
Discrimination
About people of other races
In the nation.
These people should pay
For all the hurt that they have caused.
We shouldn't have to take
The abuse any more.

Verbal and physical
Are types of this abuse,
For this behaviour
There is not an excuse.
People are scared
Of being hurt in this way,
They shouldn't have to take
The cruel things these people say.

Everyone should be able
To be who they want to be,
Not being scared
Of people who cannot see
That colour doesn't matter
We are all the same inside,
And by this rule,
The whole country should abide.

Samantha Tresler (14)

A Tale Of Vindaloo Curry

There was a young man from Surrey,
Who loved to eat vindaloo curry,
One day he ate the lot
And found out it was very hot,
So he ran to the tap in a hurry.

The same young man from Surrey,
Then he began to worry,
His tongue was all scorched
And his intestines were torched,
All for a vindaloo curry.

Mark Dowd (14)

ME

I am me, nobody else
I see others as they think they should be.
I see other people changing around me,
But I don't change, I stay the same.
I look to one side and I see the elders,
I look to the other side and I see the young,
I look to the middle and I see me,
Not me to be,
Not me then,
Just me.
I am me, nobody else.
On the inside I stay the same,
On the outside I change,
But whatever happens,
I am me,
Just me.

Chantelle Lederer (13)

FRIENDSHIP

When I think of good times,
I think of all my friends.
If we have a fall-out,
Our friendship always mends.

There's Calie and Paula
And Jessica too,
Tom, Crossy,
No one called Sue.

We like to go up town
And we like to hang about,
When we are giddy,
We run, scream and shout.

If one of us is lonely,
The rest of us are there
To cheer each other up,
To show we care.

Leanne Noble (13)

SUFFER

I sit alone
In this darkened, black cave,
The grey rocks
On both entries are blocked.
I can see
It's all too dark,
But that isn't the only thing
I need to worry about.
Air, oxygen, breath.
My oxygen is lessening
While being trapped in this cave.
I can't breathe.
All the non-existent air is choking me,
Choking me to death,
A slow, painful death.
I've been here for hours
Just waiting for my painful death,
Waiting for the lights to go out for good,
But when I die in this suffering,
I'll always remember
That my last thought
Was of me dying alone.

Irene Plunkett (16)

BAD THINGS

I was sick of looking back at some terrible things I'd done,
With my head up high, I looked forward and tried my best to have fun.
Still there in my mind, it began to ruin my head,
It kept reminding me of the worst things,
But not the good things I've done or said.
I kept hearing my childhood laughter and watching myself cry,
Taking notice of those who dislike me and always wanting to die.
I knew I couldn't cope, I began losing control,
Life was slipping away from me; body, mind and soul.
I didn't want any of this to happen,
It shouldn't be a consequence I have to pay,
I hated going round the twist and waking up to it each day.
So I walked down the path that helped me,
Made me see fear at its kindest side,
It made me see courage and life at its best, after that I could never hide.
In my life bad things have changed now,
Things are different, so it seems,
I can keep my head up high and try to fulfil my dreams.

Natalie Gill (15)

THE SHARK

Just like icicles in the snow,
His teeth were sharp and pointed.
Like lumps of soot-black coal,
His eyes were dark and haunted.

His skin was smooth and shiny,
Just like the pads on a kitten's paw.
He glided through the water
As he headed for the shore.

Rhys John (15)

COMPLETE

I love the way your hair looks so neat,
The way your eyes sparkle so bright,
The way you smile makes me tingle with joy.
When you walk past, my heart skips a beat,
In my dreams we finally shall meet.
I know in my heart you're what makes a teenage life for me
. . . Complete.

Corin Reynolds (14)

THE LODGINGS OF ME

Ere beautiful quarters these be,
The bedroom that is of me,
Never doleful or dreary,
The lodgings of me.

Extravagant in the colour,
It portrays much valour.
'Tis my parlour,
The lodgings of me.

Work, 'tis strewn everywhere,
Ere tad unfair,
'Tis my lair,
The lodgings of me.

All about the decoration,
It is but a declaration
Of all the inspiration,
In the lodgings of me.

Now we must go, close the door
And clean the dirty floor.
Alas it is no more,
The lodgings of me.

William King (14)

UNTIL I SAW THE SEA

Until I saw the sea,
It was just the sea.
I didn't see,
All animals, shapes, colours and sizes.

I did not see the sea
Was amazingly beautiful.
It can do things
That you couldn't even imagine.

One thing I saw,
I've never seen before,
The sea is not just a bowl of water,
It is what they call the sea,

Anything you can imagine.

Stephen Tuck (13)

LIFE?

When I look, all I see
Are lonely people surround me,
Milling around with no place to go,
Swaying their bodies to and fro.
Searching for unknown bliss
To free them from their loneliness.
Empty faces looking dumb,
Acting sad and feeling glum.
Pointless repeating of daily grind,
Efforts wasted with nothing to find.
In this world of sad perfection,
Are worthless lives on reflection.
All our days we are looking for
Power, authority and lots more.
The only thing that can set us free
Are friends, family and love to be.

Ruth Logan (15)

LOVE IS . . .

Love is sharing hearts,
Love is eating strawberry tarts,
Love is swopping parts,
Love is . . .

Love is when someone's always in your head,
Love is when you're in bed,
Love is when you turn red,
Love is . . .

Love is when you get a new toy,
Love is fun and joy,
Love is when a girl finds a boy,
Love is . . .

Love is a quiet place,
Love is a pretty face,
Love is the stars in space,
Love is . . .

Sylvester Espana (11)

RACISM

Deep down inside my heart,
I feel burnt and torn apart.
All the racism going round
Screws my hopes of peace and sound.

If there was a way to help the world
And stop the hatred of others beliefs,
Then I'll be first to keep the hopes
From going down Hell's steep slopes.

And if one day that chance arises,
Then racism will near its days
And the bad will run away,
Because they will know that if the world does go good,
Then they will have no chance of living-hood.

Yunus Msayib (13)

MISS ODD BOD!

Witches are said to be strange creatures
And usually have very distinctive features.
Well, the witch I know is very odd
And I know her as Miss Odd Bod.
She is rather tall and very lean
And her eyes look extremely mean.
Her face is covered in warts and zits
And all different disgusting bits,
From wrinkles and spots to flaky skin,
A beauty contest she could not win.
Her hands are bony and gnarled
And every heavily piled
With scars, blotches and holes,
Scratches, pimples and moles.
Her legs are knobbly and hairy
And if I was to touch them,
I would find it scary.
Her feet look mouldy and old
And I wouldn't touch them for a million pieces of gold.
Her hair is straggly and greasy
And the disgusting part is, her scalp
Is swarmed with many species,
Such as spiders, nits, flies and lice
And her toes are bitten by little mice.
So that's Miss Odd Bod for you,
Beware: never be there when she is baking her brew!

Elizabeth Coop   (13)

SNOW!

Snow is fun to play in, until your hands and feet go numb.
Snow comes in different shapes and sizes.
I've never been able to hold a snowflake for a long time,
Maybe because my hands are always too warm.
Snow is white,
Some snow is black,
Some snow is brown and some snow is yellow.
When it snows it covers everything,
It's fun to wake up and look out on all the snow,
Hoping that school will be closed.
Sledging down hills, having snowball fights but then,
When we are all sleeping, someone comes
And takes all the snow away!
The next morning when we wake up, all excited,
We open the curtains and it's all gone!
Snow is short-lived.

Rebecca Wilson (15)

SPRINGTIME

S pring is a great time of year,
P rancing lambs in fields near,
R abbits hopping all around,
I nnocent flowers spread across the ground,
N ever-ending colour in sight,
G reat, even when day turns to night.
T roubles and worries just fade away,
I n a great, springtime day,
M isunderstandings and arguments can be forgotten,
E ven if before you were feeling rotten.

Harriet Dineen (13)

WHEN I GROW UP

When I grow up,
I want a job to be proud of,
A job to show who I am.

When I grow up,
I want to be a teacher,
Somebody to learn from.

When I grow up,
I want to be a nurse,
Somebody to help others.

When I grow up,
I want to be a vet,
Somebody to give animals a voice.

When I grow up,
I want to be in the army,
Somebody to defend their country.

When I grow up,
I want to help,
Help everyone.

Samantha Spence (13)

FRASER WITH RAZOR

(From your favourite little niece, Julie)

I once had an uncle called Fraser,
I don't think he knew what to do with a razor.
He washed his hands,
He washed his face,
He started to scrape along his face.
My favourite auntie, my Auntie Sue,
Came bursting in to go to the loo.
My uncle jumped and the razor flew,
It flew so far it landed in the loo.
My uncle said, 'For goodness sake,
I've only scraped half of my face.'
My uncle went to the nextdoor neighbour
And asked if he could borrow a razor.
He tried to pull the other hairs out,
But he ended up with only one eyebrow.
He came up to see us the other week
And my auntie said he looked like a one-eyed freak.
As we're coming to the end of
Fraser and the razor,
I would just like to say that he's got a new razor.

Julie Brown (13)

LONELINESS

Loneliness is a sea of blue silk waving in the wind,
You are drifting along in a small boat,
You see nothing,
You hear nothing.
Loneliness is a sea of blue silk waving in the wind,
You sail along for hours and days,
The sun beaming down on you.
You have no food,
You have no drink.
Loneliness is a sea of blue silk waving in the wind,
You see no boats,
You see no people,
There is nowhere to go, except forward,
If you turn back there is nowhere to go.
Loneliness is a sea of blue silk waving in the wind,
Nightfall comes,
The moon is a silver mist among the cloudy skies.
The stars are tiny jewels hidden, not wanting to be seen,
The sea turns and becomes a rushing tornado,
The once subtle wind becomes fierce,
It's like a thousand pins being stabbed into body and face.
Loneliness is a sea of blue silk waving in the wind,
Suddenly all is calm, all is gone,
The sun is out and it's drizzling rain.
A rainbow has appeared in the sky; it's the symbol of joy
                                    and happiness,

You see boats,
You see people,
All is well and good.
Loneliness is a sea of blue silk waving in the wind.

Christine Wilcox (13)

ONE MAN . . . ONE MOMENT

The happiest moment of life
Is the peace all around,
In war-trodden countries
Of the light of hope, casting down.

The metal ton-weights
Crashing into the ground,
The screams and the wails
And the dead bodies being found.

The sneers and the laughter
Of the planners as they see
The destruction they started,
To fill their wretched hearts with glee.

One man it takes
To speak out the truth,
One moment in time
To stop the bitter feuds.

These days are tense,
The acid rivalries, long fought
And the repeated disputes.
But remember this,
Each one of you,
One man it takes,
One moment in time,
To stop all the feuds
That the earth-filled life may produce.

Jesse Panthagani (14)

UNTITLED

Everything seems pointless, empty, abandoned,
I'm lacking determination, my emotional drive shrivelled
And died, what seems like so long ago.
With every tear that falls from my eyes, a corner of my hope dies.
Never rely on me to follow through, don't depend on me,
I won't help you, I won't be there.
I can't, I can't remember how.
If the only abnormality is the incapacity to love,
Then I might as well lie down now.
My heart's hollowed out, cold.
I can't trust you or love you because I don't want to
And I can't remember how.
My past, the hurt that lives behind me,
That nagging pain in the back of my mind,
The one I've tried to bury,
Tried to smother,
The one that never dies,
It won't let me, I can't remember how.
My past did that, blocked off my trust, made me forget.
Now I can't remember how.
How to be there,
How to love you,
How to put my trust in you,
How to stop this feeling,
How to live.

Hayley Willett (15)

SHADOWS OF HAPPINESS

It's me, the girl who has everything,
The clothes; the house; the brains;
The holidays and the money,
But not the happiness.
It's the old cliché -
Money can't buy you happiness.
And it's true.
I feel
Isolated,
Inadequate and
Inconsequential,
There's nothing to free me
From the shackles of self-doubt
Because the clothes; the house; the brains;
The holidays and the money
Are all shadows of happiness.

Zoe Hurst (15)

REFUGEE

Bang, crash,
Here we go again.
'Duck for cover!'
Hiding under the table,
I'm 4 years of age.
War.
A scream,
My mum,
I cry she's gone,
All that I have left of her is an arm.
'Get out,'
My brother,
We ran to try to get to the boat.
Another crash,
Something warm and slimy on my back,
Blood.
My brother is gone too,
Just me now,
Crying, all alone.
I ran to the boat
Hoping wherever I go next
Is a better place than this.
Crying, with no family,
I curled up to keep warm.

Laura Whitbread (14)

COMPLETELY UNIFORM

The bell rings out, the school begins to crowd,
A rush of girls that chatter in their high, loud voices,
A swarm of boys that mumble, don't speak loud,
Each one the same, each in their own position,
Completely uniform.

And what's wrong if you're just not quite the same?
Your hair's not up, you haven't the right smile
Or if you won't play tradition's game?
I want to be different, not just like them,
Completely uniform.

I might talk like the girls, brazen and high
But I don't like make-up, jewellery, looking cool
Or flirting and hurting and nose up high,
That's just what they seem like,
Completely uniform.

I'm a runner, a laugher, I like climbing and sailing,
Hunting and hiding, watching football from home,
Trying and succeeding, or trying and failing,
Not trying and *stopping,* like those that are
Completely uniform.

So accept it, watch me and accept me,
I *won't* put my hair up, I *won't* smile or flirt,
I like what I like, that's how it's gonna be,
I'm individual, I just won't be
Completely uniform.
Are you?

Rosemary Pritchard (13)

YEAR ELEVEN TRAUMA!

Exam time is here
The one occasion we all fear,
Summer may be here, but no fun,
There is last minute revision to be done.

When the dreaded days loom,
All that races through the mind is doom.
What if I don't pass?
Would a whole two years be a farce?

In the exam hall the panic sets in,
What if I don't remember the deadly sins?
I rush to capture all in my mind,
But the answers become hard to find.

Results day is looming ahead,
All I want to do is crawl into bed,
But I get up and put on a brave face,
Wishing I was any other place.

All results have arrived!
Some people feel deprived,
There is heartache and joy,
I just feel sorry for a year ten boy!

Lisa Higenbottam (15)

BULLYING!

You can hit me all you like
With your stiff, broad hands.
You can jerk my greasy, blonde hair,
Let me wilt away like sand,
But still like glass, I'll shine.

Does my independence irritate you?
Why aren't you constantly penitent?
'Cause I sing like I've got humming birds,
Picking up your scent.

Just like oceans and ships,
With the certainty of tides,
Just like seas glistening bright,
Still I'll shine.

Leaving behind beatings and slaps,
I shine.
Into an evening dotted with stars,
I shine.
Bringing the hopes and dreams ashore,
I am the victim of bullies no more,
I shine,
I shine,
I shine.

Hannah Rowson (14)

IN THE PLAYGROUND

In the playground . . .
I used to shout, scream,
I was having so much fun
It felt like I was in a dream!

In the playground . . .
I used to jump and jog,
I even used to sit on a log.

In the playground . . .
I used to get told off,
While others used to sneeze and cough.

In the playground . . .
I used to see and hear the birds tweeting
High in the sky and flying by.

How could I have kept my playground quieter?
Could you have helped me?

Carla Ingamells (13)

NOT SO BAD

Everybody's hurting,
They think it'll never cease
And all my friends are suicidal,
Just trying to find some peace.
But there's always someone with me,
Someone to catch me when I fall.
You can complain, but I'll abstain,
Life's not so bad after all.

Everybody's aching
From the work they do all day,
But they won't let me help them,
As if they want to be that way.
But there's always someone with me,
Someone to catch me when I fall.
You can complain, but I'll abstain,
Life's not so bad after all.

I'll find a way to show them
All they have, all they can be,
How much everybody loves them
And maybe then they'll see
That there's always someone with them,
Someone to catch them when they fall.
They won't complain, they'll abstain,
Life's not so bad after all.

Rachel Wake (15)

MORNING TILL LUNCH

I arrived at school on the dot,
Put my plastic card in the register slot,
I am ready now with determination,
As I proceed to my station.

I switch on my computer in the usual way,
The screen on the monitor says, 'Good day,'
It displays my work,
It does not want me to shirk.

I work all morning on my computer,
Then fax my work to my tutor,
At 12 o'clock I shut down my machine
And make my way to the canteen.
I press a few buttons and turn a wheel
And out comes a healthy, low fat meal.

I work in the mornings until lunch,
Sometimes I feel like having some brunch,
When my day's work is over, I go to my crib
And for dinner, I'll have fat-free rib.

Anthony Daniel (13)

THE WORLD'S HEART

The music of the world is dying,
The jigsaw is falling apart,
What has happened to this world?
Where is its heart?

Leaving this world in such a mess
For our children to clean,
Give peace a chance
And let the love be seen.

Let the innocent live free lives,
Let us all be free,
Give our children happy lives
And help them to see.

The light of our lives,
Don't let it die,
Appreciate the world and
Look after our land, sea and sky.

Laura Gyles (13)

SPOTS AND BRACES

Get up and out of bed!
The first thing out was a spotty head.

The bathroom engaged with my brother Ben,
I don't believe it! he used my Oxyten.

Then the mood kicked in
And I ran downstairs and stood on a pin.

I screamed when I saw my brother's mates,
'My braces!' then I looked up and saw their horrifying faces.

They never came back to my house
After seeing my ugly face!

Lucy Musgrave (13)

I HATE YOU

I hate you.
Your eyes are like pools of ice,
Your skin like a pale shell.
I hate you.
Your mouth is as big as London,
Your hair like mushed banana.
I hate you.
Your head as empty as ghost towns,
Your mind like a tornado - upside down.
I hate you.

Kimberley Peacock (13)

NO ANSWER!

My heart cries out but no one seems to hear,
You seem to be so far and yet so near.
It shouts and calls your name, but you're not there
And yet I smile, without a care.
I close my eyes to imagine your face
And I see that same old familiar place.
I miss your happy smiles and your joyful laugh,
You lay there still, yet your soul walked the path.
I miss the way you lived life to the full,
You always smiled, even when times were dull.
But now I've learnt how much I love you,
I love you much more than I ever knew.
And even though my heart cracks with the pain,
I'll love and miss you 'til we meet again.

Rebekah Higgins (14)

WAR

I am a child of fantasy
I will never come to be,
Because my parents will not conceive me
Into a land that isn't free.

I know only pain, death and hatred,
I live in a world full of war,
It seems that we have forgotten
What we have been given life for.

There are no trees, hills or flowers,
Just masses of bodies and ash
The floor is burning concrete,
I can't remember fresh grass!

The air is filled with black poison
There are no longer birds in the sky
We are killing ourselves off
The planet will wither and die.

I pity the newborn babies,
Who will only know anger and pain
We have all destroyed our own planet
Our history has been in vain!

Our souls are sucked out by this hatred,
Our brains have been smothered by gas
We feel trapped inside our own bodies
Is freedom too much to ask?

Robyn Bertram (13)

THE BALLAD OF A NOBODY

The children in the school
Had never much to say
They got on with their own lives
They didn't feel his feelings each day.

He would wander round the school yard
Alone and full of grief
He had once known a somebody
But the encounter had only been brief.

He had memorised their faces
Their ages and their names
He looked at each with wonder
He had always shared their pains.

For just a glance of notice
What he wouldn't give
For people just to notice him
To acknowledge his talents . . . if . . .

But they gave him no attention
And didn't seem to look twice
They didn't acknowledge his talents
They were never friendly or nice.

Maybe if they had noticed him
He wouldn't have strayed away
He could have been so wonderful
They could have made him stay.

Rachel Denton (13)

EARTH, WIND, FIRE, WATER

Water on hand to ease starched nerves
Topping up on stamina preserves
As you embark on reliving the school year
Cramming for hours, never seeming to get near.

Earth for the mud and dirt you scuff
Dragging your heels in a depressed huff
As you wait heavy with pressure outside of the door
Retelling statistics and equations to the corridor floor.

Fire for the minutes left on the clock
When your brain's curdled and your body in shock
Looking through your work, re-scanning every word
Your stomach is churning for when the bell is heard.

Wind for the moment you stride out of the hall
Stress blowing by as you hear a friend's call
You chatter of exam questions, no nerves are mentioned
You feel happy, relieved in the exam hall congestion
As you realise the hellish sacrifices you've made
Are all worth the chance of a heaven-sent grade!

Virginia Hancock (15)

CHRISTINA

Christina's my idol,
Although she's a girl.
They say she's a slag,
But I think she's cool.
Her inspiring songs lead right to my heart,
I'd love to meet her in the flesh
And introduce her to my family.
I wish I could show her the website I've made,
I'm sure it wouldn't let her down.
From the first moment in 1998,
She touched me then and astounds me now.
I don't know what I'd do without her.
We should do a duet,
Maybe soon,
Some day,
I'll get a chance to tell her how I feel.

Danny Patrick (13)

I WONDER . . .

I wonder what life will be like in years to come.
Will people be happy or will they be glum?
Will life have changed and people too
Or will people walk around without a clue?

I wonder if there will be a war?
Power is like drugs, you just want more.
A part of me is feeling scared,
Those egotistic terrorists, they don't even care.

Will children be safe to walk to the shops?
Or will they have to hold hands with a cop?
I wonder if crime levels will decrease
And will people be able to sleep with ease?

Will people be in cars or flying spaceships?
Or will they be in rockets, waiting for an eclipse?
I wonder if trains will exist any more
Or will we just have memories of train carriage doors?

The future seems close, yet so far away,
Will life be precious or just treated as another day?
Will people value all that they use?
Life will probably just be abused.

Natasha Hussein (13)

HOPE

A light shines from beneath the door
An echo of a broken child screaming, 'Please no more.'
I never want to dwell on the pain again,
A memory of how you kept me so afraid.
There was no one else I couldn't look inside myself.

How I used to gasp for air and cry in despair,
I thought I would grow scared, too afraid
And run out of faith, I'm happy for the courage I have gained.

I hope some day I find my brighter day
And find the right path and be on my way.

Alana Hanley (14)

CHILDREN OF THE SKY

Shifting effortlessly,
Endless asymmetrical patterns,
Born from foamy, dull, grey wombs,
A pathetic source of light
Lays in wait
For a suitably thin infant
To penetrate and reach the dull rooftops
Of a tired earth.

Stirring, like thieves in shadows,
Like a dreaming baby,
Somersaulting, floating, travelling like distant fairies,
Concealing an unknown world,
The infants continue on their uncertain path,
On their endless journey.

Jonathan Cole (14)

No Time To Care Or Look About

People have no time nowadays,
To watch nature or stand and gaze.
We traipse around not caring where we run
We think killing animals is jolly good fun.
We don't mind if we pollute the air
Or drop litter here and there.
As long as the money comes pouring in,
We don't mind if what we do is a sin.
People have no time nowadays,
To watch nature or stand and gaze.
Not to listen to the birds
Or help a friend
We destroy things and don't make amends.

Mariessa Joseph (13)

MY LIFE

Why is my life so complicated?
That I do not know
When I look at others
I wonder why mine can't be like theirs?

Out till late
Doing what they want
Compare that to my life
Why do I have no freedom?

In at seven
Bed at half past nine
What life is this
For someone of my age?
That I do not know.

My mum doesn't understand
She thinks seven is a perfectly reasonable time to get in
Why doesn't she get it, why doesn't she understand?

One day I'll be like them, stayin' out all night,
Having a laugh, doing what I want, *wow* that sounds cool
Why can't my life be like that now?
That I do not know.

But one thing I do know is that my parents care about me
My life might not be the best
But hey, at least I'll get a good job when I'm older.

Elaine Lunt (14)

JOURNEY THROUGH THE MIND OF A TEENAGER

I dodge the *Danger, No Entry* signs
And down I spiral
Into the murky depths of the bottomless pit.
In and out of the labyrinth of endless tunnels
Of helpless homeworks
And useless information, diligently learnt.

I spin around the corner and am
Catapulted into a capacious chasm of cerebration
As memories dart past me
I catch a glimpse of
A sunset stroll on a soft, sandy shore,
A triumphant tale of a turbulent victory
And the innocence of childhood
Merged into the intimidating prospect of the 'real world'.

Deeper I plunge
Into the icy currents of the tempestuous flood,
A cacophony of sounds erupting around me
As faces whirl past; family, friends and
Despised enemies locked inside this
Chest of treasures
For all eternity.

And suddenly I am lost
In the blackened swamp of emotion;
The painful yearn of love, lost and found
And the electrifying sensation of success,
The dark chill of pain and suffering
And the bitter stains of envy and hatred.
But even deeper lies the pure, white light
Of courage and determination
Lighting our way.

Joanne Box (14)

WHY WAR?

Why should we go to war?
Why should there be pain and suffering
Why should the world be hungry?
Why can't everyone get along?
Why should there be a war?

Zoë Viner (14)

TEENAGE PLEA!

Give me strength,
Give me power,
Give me money by the hour.

Make me happy,
Give me friends,
Give me a love that never ends.

I want no pain,
I want no heartache,
But, please Mum, just give me a break!

Gemma Connell (13)

WHAT AM I GONNA DO?

I'm 13 years old
What am I gonna do?
I hate going to school
I'm always in trouble
What am I gonna do?

I love playing football
I sometimes score goals
But not in the right net
What am I gonna do?

I would like to be 18
Then I could leave school
I could get a job
What am I gonna do?

Jamie Selby (13)

THE BROKEN CHILD

I am the broken child,
Do not try to comfort me,
Stay away so eyes don't see,
What wraps me in misery.
Do not touch,
Go away,
Say goodbye to yesterday.

Faye Burrows (14)

MONEY

Money's good,
Money's bad,
Money is something
Poor people never had.
The women like to spend it
Around the shops,
Buying different shoes,
Buying different tops.
The men go and waste it,
Down the pub,
Drinking a load of beer
Or even in a club.
But kids enjoy it the most,
It makes them feel free,
Deep down inside what we care about the most
Is our friends and family.

Rebecca Moore (13)

SLOWLY FALLING APART

The world seems so small,
Nowhere to hide or run,
Buildings start to crumble around me,
Noise of shattering glass surrounds me,
Screams of those in pain, ring in my ears like a telephone
I feel little and helpless,
Tears running down my cheeks like a tap which has been left on
No one to go to
Feel my heart tearing inside me.

Nowhere to hide or run,
Feeling that the world is against you
Everything or everyone you seem to touch, hurt you little by little
The walls outside start to close in on you.

Your throat slit open,
Your heart sliced in two,
Start to find it hard to breathe
Oh the suffering is making me grow weaker
There is no medicine which can be prescribed for this.

There is nowhere to hide or run
The damage is done
Sooner or later I shall get my revenge.

Seema Syed (15)

If

If you do not love me,
I understand.
If you do not want me,
I'll go.
If you need to talk,
I'll be there.
If you need a friend,
I'll be next door.
If you do not want me in your life,
I'll turn around and walk away.
If you fall,
I'll be there to help you get back up.
If you are sad,
I'll be there so you can cry on my shoulder.
If you ever need me,
I'm never far.
I'm always around,
To look after you.

Alex Baker (14)

LIFE IS NOT FAIR

When a teenager's appearance needs to be cool,
Why does Mother Nature have to be so cruel?
Just when you need to impress your mates
And look presentable for your dates.

Greasy hair, blotchy acne and numerous spots,
You look in the mirror and you've got the lot,
Smelly, sweaty armpits and a pizza face,
Sprouting embarrassing hairs all over the place.

Feelings are prickly, emotions run really high,
Moods swing to and fro and you don't know why,
Parents are aliens - they certainly have never been,
An angry, confused person in their teens.

The body develops at an alarming rate,
A squeaky voice that we really hate,
Raging hormones, a tantrum here and there,
All we can say is, *life is not fair!*

Mark Chew (14)

MY VIEW

Why does it matter if you're black or white?
Who's the judge, who decides?
Different cultures and religions fight
When does it stop, why can't it end?
When will we eventually see that each individual should be free?
Everyone has the right to live in harmony
So why can't we?

Louise Warden (13)

No Money!

I'm desperate for some money
My mum thinks it's so funny
I want to buy that new bag
Oh my God, have you seen the price tag
There is no money in my purse
It just can't get much worse
I need some money on my phone
My mum says I shouldn't moan.

Lucy Graven (14)

THE TEENAGE YEARS

The teenage years are full of perplexity
A million emotions in your mind
All you feel is ambivalence
You were told no, but you do it anyway
You have repented again.

The teenage years are full of stress
There are a million things you have to do
You feel your frustration intensify
You want to be left alone
So you can sulk in peace.

The teenage years are full of fun
Your social life is full to bursting
So much to do, so little time
But how on earth can you decide
Between a sleepover and a shopping trip?

The teenage years are full of changes
You make new friends
You learn new things
You discover what it's like to fall in love
And most importantly, who you are.

Rebecca Groves (14)

SUICIDE

Into my veins the blade cuts in deep
To make me fall into a never-ending sleep
Where I want to stay asleep and never wake up
While the blood pours out of me like water into a cup.

The room spins round as I fall to the ground
All I want to do is kill the monster in my head
But all I'm doing is killing me instead.

My arms I can no longer feel
But this all seems so unreal
I can feel pain all over me
Even though nothing I cannot see
As my spirit comes out of me
I come out of myself.

I've changed my mind, I want to live,
What I've done is wrong
As I die I hear my sister's radio
Playing her favourite song.

All my blood rushes out
Then I hear my mother's shout
In the red puddle as I lay on the floor
I hear a knock at the door
But it's too late, I've gone
Nothing can bring me back now.

Penny Lane (14)

MY POEM

Some people think we're moody,
Some people think we're punks,
They think the guys just want the babes
And they think the girls want hunks,
Well let me say that they are wrong,
What they say is just untrue,
We're not all rowdy troublemakers
Us teens are people too!
Don't assume we're always drunk,
Shoplifting or starting fights,
Not every young person is the same
We too have our rights!

Claire Donbavand (13)

TRENCHES

Why did I come to this horrible place?
To see my friends with a tattered face.
The trenches are full of mud and water,
While day-by-day I hear the blast from a mortar.

In the trenches I worry about the rats,
Because some of them are as big as cats.
We don't get enough food a day,
Which goes along with our poor pay.

Day by day my trench foot is getting worse,
So I wish I had someone to treat it like a nurse.
At any moment I could stick a knife in my foot and feel no pain,
But if it wasn't for my dear friend I would go completely insane.

My friend is a victim of severe shell-shock,
I wish I could turn back time on my clock.
All my companions are fading away,
O please help me God as I lay down and pray.

Richard Bainbridge (14)

SCHOOL AND EXAMS

If only school was fun,
We could learn a lot more,
If only there were less exams,
We would have a stress-free life.

School is what you make it, fun, fun, fun,
The years at school are meant to be the best,
We only remember the happy times, and
We make the sad times slip away.

Exams are sent to test and try us,
They are used for us to learn
We pass with flying colours,
We fail with a frown.

School has many meanings,
We have terms and holidays, to give us a break,
We are at school for 12 years
Some do more, some do less.

Exams have a number of results,
We take study leave in Year 11,
We sit four stages, 1, 2, 3 and GCSE,
Some do more if they stay on at school.

If only we stayed at school longer,
We would learn more and work less
One set of exams would be enough
We would have less stress and more fun.

Lena Robinson (14)

LIFE IS LIKE A METAPHOR

Like a dagger
Or a knife
Able to slice
The fear of death
Into anyone,
Anything.

Inanimate objects
Are impenetrable
By the knife
Protected against death
And suffering
Fearless.

If losing the knife
Means certain death
But keeping it
Presents only a risk
And it's stolen
Injustice.

Living organisms
Are vulnerable
When the knife
Is sharp
And your life is good,
Never-ending.

Emma Bramley (15)

MANCHESTER UNITED

My favourite footie team is Manchester United
And they've beaten every team that's ever been sighted!
Barthez is loony, Beckham's a star
And Van Nistelrooy never misses and never hits the bar.
Penalties are taken, free kicks are scored
And corners are whipped in and Scholes's always there to score.
Old Trafford is where the magic happens
No matter what kit they're playing in red, white or blue
There's always someone to head one in
And who knows one day it might be you!
Forlan was a bit dodgy at first
And it seemed like years before he'd score
But in one game he grabbed a penalty
And how he's gonna get one every day
Manchester United my favourite footie team.

Scott Proctor (14)

TEENAGER'S WORRIES

I am so fat,
I am so ugly,
I look like a bat,
My spot looks like a bogey.

My breasts are small,
My teeth are wonky,
I am just too tall
And my face, my face looks like a donkey.

I have never had a boyfriend,
I have new smells,
Boys drive me round the bend,
Sweat drops like bells.

No one rings me,
What have I done wrong?
My friend's ringtones sound like a bee,
Should I wear a thong?

I think I need an inflatable bra,
I don't want to be me
Or maybe have a day in the spa,
Oh God help me!

Jenny Kendal (13)

HIS HOUSE

I
left
his house
clutching my
reading and a
tissue, I'd just been
speaking to a gathering
and the writing on my paper
had been about her, but she is
now with him doing whatever
she wants, so I can't see her anymore
'cause she is nowhere to be found, except
in the grass, the trees, the water and all the
things she used to love, but I will get to see
her, not too soon I hope, because I want to
have this part of life for a long time on
Earth and then be put in a space around
his house with someone else doing my
reading and then I can go up to see
her and we can do all
the things we used
to love.

Cara Edwards (14)

I'M LYING SICK IN MY BED ...

I'm lying sick in my bed,
Wondering what to do.
Thoughts running through my head
Not a lot to do.
Here I am coughing and sneezing,
Not a lot to do.
My head's pounding like someone's shouting,
But there's nothing I can do.
I'm lying sick in my bed,
Wondering what to do.

I'm lying sick in my bed,
Wondering what to do.
Beside me, my friend, Big Ted,
Not a lot to do.
Taking tablets and watching TV
Not a lot to do.
Can't go to school to do PE
But there's nothing I can do.
I'm lying sick in my bed,
Wondering what to do.

Carly Butterworth (14)

MY WORLD

My world is adventurous full of trouble and friends,
I mostly live in harmony, but I often hit dead ends,

I get into a lot of mischief all day and night it's true,
My family say I've bitten off more than I can chew,

I like a bit of laughter to bring colour to my life,
But half the time my life goes dull, like stabbing with a knife,

My world in time goes up and down like a bouncing ball
And even sometimes upside down like hanging off a wall,

Every day is a new adventure, just waiting to be found,
In the bubbling waters or even on the ground,

My world is open to anyone, but you'll surely get a fright,
I'm mixed-up with all emotions and my heart is made of light.

Carly Hawkes (13)

OLLIE THE CAT

Ollie is a cat
Who is rather fat
He's black and white
And sometimes gives you a fright
He once got knocked over
And couldn't then walk far
So he went to the vet
Then ran as fast as a jet
Then it happened a second time
People would think he's trying to commit a crime
Now he walks in the garden
And has a little pen
Some people call it his little den
That's our pet, he's called Ollie
He makes us all proud and jolly.

Samantha Grummitt (13)

TEENAGERS WANNA HAVE FUN

Our parents say we give too much cheek
But really we're just being cool and sleek
Shouting to get us off the phone
Never happy, just moan and groan.

When we want to go out, late at night,
They shout and scream and start a fight
'You're not going out in that, it's far too revealing!'
We make them so angry, they hit the ceiling.

We're the reason they hit the bottle
Soon our necks, they'll throttle
Apparently hormones fly everywhere
Maybe that's why they pull out their hair.

And then we want to go on our first date
But this question has a deadly fate
'No way, you're far too young!'
Teenagers can't do right by doing wrong.

They say they were our age as well
But they insist to make our lives hell!
We all love our parents a ton
But teenagers just wanna have fun.

Emma Campbell (13)

COOL SCHOOL

Everyone goes to school,
People say it's not cool,
In my free time all I do is talk,
I go outside and go for a walk,
I always try my best,
When I go home I just totally rest,
Loads of people come in late,
Except for me and my best mate,
Lunchtime comes, there's loads of food,
When there's nothing left everyone goes in a mood,
At the end of the day you can guess,
Who makes all the mess!

Tiffany Roberts (13)

IN MY HEAD

Nobody's head is quite the same as mine.
First there's my family and friends
And the mountain of homework that never ends
Next my self defence,
I keep that at the back
In the dark, until Tuesdays,
Then it will spark.
Next my pets,
The cats, the fish and the guinea pig.
My boyfriend Ross who is so sweet and never cross
My friend Chantelle who can always tell what I am thinking,
She's my best friend right from the beginning.
So that is a journey around my brain
And nobody's brain is ever the same.

Cassie Brown (15)

POEM

A teenager is like the weather, changing every day.
One minute up, the next minute down, from April through to May.

A teenager can be like a poem, joyful, funny and calm.
Just chilling out, doing nowt, with a sweaty left palm.

If you look at photos, of when you were a kid.
You'll see how much you've changed, you've been totally rearranged
But you'll never be able to close the lid.

All teens like different things, whether it's football to hockey,
Playing music, chasing girls or even being soppy.

Everyone is unique, they have their special ways
From being sad to happy and glad, this is all you need to say.

Thomas Hamer (13)

WHAT I FEEL

It's eleven minutes past three
As I sit in front of the TV
With a pencil in my hand
And paper on my lap
Thinking what to write
How to express, what I'm feeling in my mind;
But regardless of my efforts
The words don't emerge
And happiness seems a distant memory
As tears roll down my cheeks, incessantly.

What I feel inside
Isn't easy to describe
An emptiness in my stomach, a hole inside my heart
Loneliness and dismay, that I encounter
Each and every day
A yearning to be distinguished
To turn my aspirations into reality;
But until that day arrives
I shall learn to be proud of who I am
And strive to achieve my hopes and dreams.

Donya Fredj (15)

FRIENDS!

Friends are the most important people to care for in your life,
Can you imagine life without them?
No friends,
That would be horrible,
Who would you laugh with?
Who would you cry with?
Who would you gossip with?
Oh no, I don't want to know the answers,
What about the bullies?
Would they hurt you?
Would they call you names?
Of course they would,
As they have no friends of their own,
That's why they bully you for,
Best to have friends,
Which care for you,
When you are hurt,
When you laugh and
When you cry and
Of course to be there for you forever
Thank God I have friends,
Have you got any friends?

Rosie Powell (14)

MY OWN WORLD

Sometimes I drift into my own world,
Away from the sea of the nameless faces,
The anger and the fighting stops
And none of the same old boring places.

In my world there is no noise or sound,
No blackened-out windows,
There are always blue clouds.

All suffering stops, it comes to an end,
So I trust my own world,
My home, my friend.

Rebecca Towers (13)

GUIDANCE THROUGH LIFE

You are the light that guides me,
Through the darkness paths I go,
You are the oceans and all seven seas,
You are the rain, the wind and the snow.

You are the rivers that make the dry damp,
You tell me the right things to do
For you are my spirit that guides me in life,
You're my strengths and my weakness too.

You are the mountains I must climb,
You trust when no one believes,
Yet inside my heart I'll always know,
That you are what my life conceives.

Lauren Thornton

WAR

We are going to war
And that is for sure,
All that trouble and strife
And wasted life.

Does nobody care
What will happen out there?
When the first plane will fly
And the first child will cry?

The word strikes fear,
Into those who are near,
To where it will be,
Scared of what they will see.

Has nothing been learned,
Nor no wisdom earned,
From wars of the past,
How long will this last?

We all want wars to cease,
But most we want peace,
So the world can join hands
And spread happiness through the lands.

Many wars have gone past,
They will not be the last,
But as wars have gone by,
There is still one unanswered question . . .
Why?

Sarah Entwistle (14)

WHEN YOU LEFT (FAREWELL)

You've gone, gone like the wind
You got up and left
Like there's nothing to keep you
I watched you leave, not a care in the sky
I'm telling you, it put a tear in my eye.

Come back and visit whenever you can
I don't care when or where or how!
As long as you are here
That will do fine
As long as you're with me, your hand in mine.

Sarah Greenwood (13)

EMINEM!

He's the world's greatest rapper
He doesn't wear clothes made by Kappa
He has got his own movie
He uses no words like groovy
His lyrics are packed with swear words
But his fans still come in herds
He dances on stage
But he has so much rage
He is just a white boy
Rapping in Detroit
He is just so, so mad
He didn't even know his dad
He is also part of D12
He had a hit called *Lose Yourself*
Have you guessed him?
That's right, it's Eminem.

Sam Allan

WHAT WE'RE ABOUT

We pledged allegiance to the underworld,
Once loved, but now hated by the majority,
We few stand alone, keeping our music alive,
We're singled out.

Guitar distortion rots our brains,
Our ears are finely tuned,
We've made up our minds there's no turning back,
We're singled out.

Black, red and black, our favourite colours,
We wear chains and dog collars and studded armbands,
Not forgetting hoodies and baggy jeans,
We're singled out.

Some like Blink 182 and Greenday,
Others Slipknot and Korn,
Many enjoy Offspring and Reel Big Fish,
But we're all singled out.

We all choose to be part of this minority,
We cry out, 'Down with the townies authority,
Let's make ourselves a majority,
'Cause we're part of a scary minority.'

Ben Folwell (13)

MY ROOM

My room is somewhere I can relax,
Somewhere I can escape to when my brother drives me up the wall.
Somewhere I can be on my own,
Somewhere I can think about what I want.

My room is fairly large, it isn't very small.
My room is nice and peaceful, it isn't loud at all.
I think my room is wonderful, it truly is great,
It's hand-painted by my mum, so let's all celebrate.

Samantha Redfern (13)

SPOTS

Spots are yellow, spots are red,
When you get them, you wish you were dead!
They always pop up when you've got a date
They're really annoying, you get in a state!
They're sometimes big, sometimes small,
Us teens, we get them all!
Spots are ugly, spots are sore,
You know what I mean, you've had one or more!

Terri Gray (13)

ANNOTATING POEMS

Think of the destruction,
a man's hard work,
torn apart by hordes of people,
trying to find meaning,
though the work still remains,
not much has been left,
he is told of what he thought
and his 'deeper meaning' meant.

Neil Everett (15)

TEEN

When I became a teenager I started to look at the future
Stuff started to change, my life got better, I got older and bigger
And smarter so I am just a teenager in a plain world.
Got more jobs, it got tired, got lazy, am only a teenager
Seems like a lifetime but I cannot change my life
I've got older, got more stuff and I am just fourteen.
Sometimes my mind goes back,
I forget stuff like where I've left my keys or money in my box
The other day forgot my pin number, I am so stupid.
Stupid, stupid I am only fourteen and I forget stuff what I am like.
So do not look back at the past
Look forward to the future
It brings better stuff
In my life I am not just a plain teenager.

Raymond Finn (14)

THESE MIXED-UP TEENAGE YEARS

Boys to impress
Choosing which dress
In these mixed-up teenage years

School work is hell
Hoping to do well
In these mixed-up teenage years

Pigsty for a room
Mum will give up soon
In these mixed-up teenage years

Bad attitude girl
My head's in a whirl
In these mixed-up teenage years

Crushes, exams
Mess, stress
Must be mixed-up teenage years.

Kristie Silsby (14)

?

In a hundred years:
Will there still be pain and suffering,
War and fighting,
Arguments and dispute?

In a hundred years:
Will there still be hunger,
Poverty and greed,
A need for begging and charity?

In a hundred years:
Will there still be laughter,
Fun and excitement,
Kisses and hugs?

In a hundred years:
Will the Earth still be here
Or will we destroy it?

Sarah Morgan (14)

WHY DON'T THEY UNDERSTAND?

'Hurry up, you'll be late for school,'
Uniform should be tidy, that's their rule,
'Roll down your skirt, straighten up your tie,'
'Get up,' they say, when in bed you lie.

Once you've rolled down your skirt, it looks too long,
So your tie is a little wonky, what's so wrong?
You go to school and are happy with your friends,
You get home and that fun ends.

They ask you what you've done today,
I guess that's alright in a way,
Then you get a phone call from one of your friends,
Who, what, when, where? The questions never end.

They don't understand that some things you like to keep to yourself,
Otherwise you might as well be an open book on a shelf,
You shout, scream, yell, 'Go away,'
But that doesn't help at the end of the day.

My advice to you is use the fact,
That it is wisest to think before you act.

Ceara Ovens (14)

OPTIONS

What to choose?
What to do?
Do this! Do that!
Don't do this!
Don't do that!
Options for GCSE coming soon,
Options for GCSE beginning to loom,
What to choose?
What to do?
Do this, Do that!
Don't do this!
Don't do that!
I just don't know,
It has left me feeling low,
What to choose?
What to do?
Don't do this!
Don't do that!
Such a lot of things to do,
Such a lot of thinking to do,
What to choose?
What to do?
Do this! Do that!
Don't do this!
Don't do that!
I have really lost the plot,
After doing such a lot.

Oliver Butler (13)

I LOVE YOU

I love you
But you don't love me back.
When I look forward
The future's black.
Sometimes I feel
That I'm all alone,
By myself, far from home.

When I dare,
I steal a look.
A little glance,
Behind a book.
That's when I know
What you think,
That in your heart,
I'm the missing link.

Heather Naylor (13)

TO THE SIX MILLION

That's you,
You see it? They burned it into your clothing,
That is your star of justice.

That's you,
Can't you recognise it?
You've always used it,
Now, they just want to use it too,
So they know who you are.

That's you,
They want to know whom they can swear at
On the street,
Those whose windows they can smash.

That's you,
So they know they have to take you,
When the time comes to take.
That's you, so they know whom to hate.

That's you,
You don't need to tell them a name,
Just give them a number,
The star on your sleeve will do the rest.

That's you,
So they know not to send the perfect people
Into those dry showers.

That's you,
Your flesh and your blood,
Your skin and your star,
They hate you all.
That's your name now.

Jewish child.

Sarah E Thompson

CHESS AND LIFE

Life is but a chess game
A chess game which repeats itself.

We are but pawns
Who, when we reach the other end
Become something which was lost.

No one knows how the game started.
The king is the chosen child
White king equals child of light,
Black king equals child of dark.
Both are needed for this world.

The queen is the loyal friend
The bishops are the fighters for belief
The knights are the people who jump at the chance to help
The castles are the people who build up the game.

When checkmate occurs,
The game restarts itself.

Logic is the way to play this game.

Sarah Pastuch (13)

FOOTSTEPS

I walked along the gloomy, dark lane,
My jacket clenched tightly together,
I knew the sounds I would soon hear,
The footsteps of him getting near and near.

As the road began to wind and curl
The wind began to howl,
Groaning trees commenced to sway
Urging me not to come, stay away.

The sinister sky was dim and moonless,
As I quickened my pace to a jog,
Footsteps sounded louder in my ear
Isolated, anxious, my panic sheer.

Eerie shadows were cast on the land,
Me, not noticing them, as on I ran
He was in the bushes, I could see
I was hoping he wouldn't seize me.

Light was in my view now,
I knew I was nearly there
Back to my home, my safe retreat
I am glad, my peril I did not meet.

Katharine O'Farrell (13)

BEING A TEENAGER

Being a teenager is great fun
Because now our young childhood is done.
You can go out to discos
Or buy brand new clothes
You can hang out with mates
Or you can go on romantic dates

Being a teenager can be hard
Because you get treated like a tub of lard.
You can get called names
Or be picked on in games.
You can feel bored
Or you can even get ignored.

Being a teenager can be embarrassing
Because your parents won't let you do your own thing.
You can be driven in a rusty car
Or you have to walk with your mum very far.
You can be dropped off just outside of school
And be made to look like an absolute fool.

Being called a teenager gives you a great feeling
Because you feel as high as the ceiling.
But take each day as it comes
Take your time when you climb
And eventually you will get to adulthood in good time!

Candy Bryant (13)

HEAVEN MADE COOL!

(My big brother Nom was killed in a car accident nearly a year ago,
not long after the accident I wrote this poem in memory of him,
I really miss him and this poem just shows what I'm feeling about him.
He died just months before his 21st birthday)

Where in Heaven are you Nom?
It's so sad that you've gone!
From time to time I wonder why
That I cry and cry and cry because . . .
I know that you're in a good place
I know you're not too far from space
Having fun, giggling, laughing
Jumping round like this never happened
'Cause you know we know you're safe
Resting in the heavenly place.
You watch over, smiling down
Guiding us like a shining star
Telling us in our hearts that you're
Not too far.

My brother Nom, you are so cool
Nom with your nickname too,
Your personality really ruled
Nom, Nug, I love you
Nug 4 ever!

Lucy Gibb

A Child's Wish

I wish for a time with uncontrollable peace
No guns, no war, no death
A time where men and women can be free
I wish for a time where we all can be happy
No blood, no tears
I wish for a time.
I wish for a time where no child would fear a thing
Or a place with pure joy
I wish for a time.

Ayesha Raymond (13)

WHAT'S MINE?

I'm all alone, no one's here,
They're not even slightly near,
My feelings are far away,
And maybe they'll come out one day.

Sometimes no one understands,
That I need someone to take hold of my hands,
And lead me in a new direction,
To help me make my connection.

I need to find my soul,
And dig myself out of this hole,
So help me search this universe
And free me from its curse.

Nikki Ryan (14)

WAR OVER?

At an end to a war the soldiers march home
No longer as comrades, but alone
They arrived believing that it was a game
They returned the blind, the depressed, and the lame.
They came pleasantly marching unprepared for what they saw
The number of men that returned was less than the number before
They returned bleak, hungry, woeful, and cold
Tired from the years of combat
In which they had been courageously bold
And now they were finally realising a dream
To be back home in England, and their house by the stream
They were pondering at the loss of good, brave men
With the hope that war would never happen again
For war had changed this nation but at a price that was too high
What cause could be so great that so many should die?
What cause could be so great
To cause a parent to lose the girl, their boy?
What cause could be so great that human values we'd destroy?
And for what? Because politicians and leaders cannot get along
Do we have to lose lives to learn that war is wrong?

Beth Shearing

WHAT FRIENDS SAY

Smoking's cool, say my friends,
No way, I say.
Please try, they urge. It's good.
No! No! No! I scream.
Who wants lung cancer, too die young? Not I.

Drugs are great, say my friends.
No way, I say.
Please try, they urge. It's fun.
No! No! No! I scream.
My mind's just fine, just fine.

Have some drink, one sip, say my friends.
No way, I say.
Please try, they urge. It's a laugh.
No! No! No I scream.
Don't want to be sick, fall over.

Skip classes, say my friends.
No way, I say.
Please come, they urge. Who cares.
No! No! No! I scream.
Don't want to miss out, must learn.

Smoking's cool!
Drugs are great!
Drinking is fun! Skip class, who care!
This is what friends say.

Megan McLean (13)

THE SONG OF THE FIDDLER

Oh play your song Dear Fiddler!
An elegy for woe,
Oh please serenade us Dear Fiddler!
Till all the world's sadness does go . . .

The sombre tune of the fiddler,
The music outpours from his breast,
The pluck of the strings, on his dusty violin,
Does bring back life meaning and zest.

The music does sing on the night air,
May its song spread far and wide,
Let it wash away tears, and chase away fears,
Let it live like the soul does inside . . .

Oh play your song Dear Fiddler!
An elegy for woe,
Oh please serenade us Dear Fiddler!
Till all the world's sadness does go . . .

Will the fiddlers tune take away famine?
Could it take away our plight?
Can it turn solitude, into loving brotherhood?
Can it make our wrongs turn into a right?

Ah! But no, but no, Dear Fiddler . . .
Greed does always overthrow . . .
Makes peace into war, scars the people with sores,
And laces our tears with woe . . .

Oh play your song Dear Fiddler!
An elegy for woe,
Oh please serenade us Dear Fiddler!
Till all the world's sadness does go . . .

Robbie Ramsay (13)

THE SCHOOL BULLY

Oh no, here she comes,
What will I do?
I have not brought money for her,
I'll have to run.
Too late, she's got me,
She's put me to the wall.
She says,
'Give me your dinner money!'
What will I do?
I have not got any money,
Then the bell rang.
She dropped me,
I fell to the floor.
She ran,
I was safe for now.
That's what I thought!

Emma Bunday (13)

MY TRIP TO VENUS

When I took a trip to Venus,
I sailed among the stars,
To reach this rocky planet,
There were even floating cars.

This planet was like a dream,
Fulfilling my command,
As I stepped into this world,
And onto this precious land.

As the sunrays hit my skin,
At 400°C,
The average temperature,
Oh how lucky I must be.

There were some things that were bad,
More hours in a day,
But I'm lucky being here,
That's a small price to pay.

Spinning slower and slower,
This planet was so different,
From east to west,
This planet so differently sent.

I will never forget this trip,
As it was like fame,
Being upon a different planet,
Venus was its name.

Natalie Gallagher (14)

WHEN I'M ILL

When I'm ill I stay at home,
All day long I moan and groan.
I moan at Mum, I moan at Dad,
I seem to drive everyone mad!

I lie on the sofa watching TV
Wishing I could just feel like me.
I then suddenly start to cry,
I feel like I'm going to die!

I really want to eat lots of sweets,
But Mum says I can't have any treats!
She sends me up to my bed,
But I want to play on the PlayStation instead!

Everyone keeps asking me if I feel OK,
I wish they would just go away.
At least when I'm ill, I don't go to school,
So not being well is also quite cool!

Rebecca Mortimer (13)

THE SEA WILL BECKON

The waves will tumble,
The waves fall,
Tipped with white they often call,
Their surging current does not cease.

Most say they never toy,
But all alone stands one young boy.
His voice calls out strong and clear,
'Where is everyone, can't they see,
Don't they know what's happened to me.'

Tears rolling down his face,
Walking into the water, there seems no cure.
Doom has taken his past and future.
His body slowly sinking, his hand reached out.

The waves will tumble,
The waves will fall.
Tipped with white they often call.
His body lies on the ocean floor,
Cold and hard, he's nevermore.

Sophie Moore (13)

THE SEA

The sea seizes fish,
Fish eaten by the seagulls,
Flying and guarding
For fish to jump out
Of the crystalline surface of water.
The water turns and turns
Like a whirlpool,
It grows and grows
Like the fertilised ovule
In the belly of a mother.
It roars in the middle of night,
And wakes you up.
What's happening?
The sea's waves are huge,
Lightning is visible
Far off in the distance
For instances,
Night disappears
And day is falsely present.
The sea explodes
In all is muscley power,
Against the rocks,
It turns the night
Into a colossal scene
Of massive power.

Paula Traver (13)

CALL OF THE CROW

A lone wolf on a hill,
His spirit is free,
His subtle body still,
He bounded, he leapt, now neither can he do.

The call of a crow rings clear,
Scarlet snow covers the ground,
The crow is standing near,
She smiles at a jest only the death bringer knows.

With a spark of evil in her mordant eye,
She has to cry out, foretelling a death,
Because of her voice fair creatures die,
The wolf in the snow is a victim of the call of the crow.

Black as hate, cruel as winter,
The crow atop a bare tree,
A halo of evil surrounds her,
In death she revels and her life renewed in blood.

Caitlin Powell

MY WORLD

In my world there is no war,
Peace will be my salvation,
Family my inspiration.

No guns, no knives on the streets,
Or in my existence.
I want to do well, not became a statistic of war.

Love and hope and goodwill
To all people, every nation
On our planet filled with love for each other.

I must be a child of today, a man for tomorrow
And hope there is no war.

Nathan Roberts (13)

HIGH SCHOOL
(How I feel)

Year Seven is when you're new to the school.
All you wanna do is make friends and look cool.

Year Eight is a doss year from my point of view
But if you think differently I wouldn't like to be you.

Year Nine you make your choices and all stuff like that.
It is also important because you do your SATs.

Year Ten you're doing your subjects that you chose last year.
All this and good GCSEs will help you with your career.

Year Eleven is test time again but make sure you keep your cool
And remember this is it! Then you'll be leaving school!

Jade Newns (14)

TEENAGE TROUBLES

You feel like you're trapped with nowhere to go,
You worry about school and feel really low.
Spots arise all over your face,
But everyone matures at their own pace.

You start to smell, get stressed too,
Remember it's not just happening to you.
There's people to talk to, so get it off your chest,
Don't let it get you down, feel the best.

Yelling at your parents is what it's all about,
Those horrible hormones make you scream and shout.
Some people even get bullied too!
Well that's tough teenage life for you!

Sarah Phillips (13)

PICTURE SO PERFECT

Shadows on the bushes
Signpost to nowhere
Barns full of nothing
Cat's eyes that stare
Snow on the hills
Sun shining through
Isolated houses
Horizon is fading.

Songs on the radio
Plane in the sky
Things that remind
Spray wash successful
Pigeons on the rooftops
The clock strikes twelve
Traffic at a minimum.

Men alone on the road
Beautiful tulips lie dead
Dreaming of a better way
And I forget to say
People don't care today
Glory streets abandoned
Broken lights ahead
Place we go is closed

Walking aimlessly
Destination nowhere
Shop selling souvenirs
Childhood memories we cherished
T-shirts with logos
Back alley full of teens
Can't feel these feelings
Not any more anyway.

Jack Conway (13)

ONE YEAR ON

One year on, we still remember,
One year on, we still feel the pain,
One year on, we still have nightmares.

One year on, we're still not satisfied,
One year on, we're still trapped,
One year on, we're still fighting.

One year on, the grief is still there,
One year on, the terrorists are still at large,
One year on, they're both still gone.

One year on, we still struggle to breathe,
One year on, people have not forgotten,
One year on, it's now Ground Zero.

One year ago we suffered,
But now the end is at a close,
And the new beginning is almost here.

Gemma Cooper (13)

BATTLES, WARS AND CONFLICTS

Terror-stricken citizens took cover
As tanks, artillery and platoons came.
The hate, the pain that citizens suffered
Were from wars and conflict, if we must blame.

Thousands of soldiers fell in battle
To save their kind in the phenomenon.
Their populous city turned to rubble,
So communities broke, families torn.

The citizens saw their relatives die;
Their fresh blood covered the barren city.
Even the invaders gave out a sigh,
'Where exactly is the humanity?'

Cease the battles, wars and conflicts I say,
Or else it will last until Judgement Day!

Hok Shun Poon

SOUNDS LIKE WAR!

The birds peacefully chirping in the trees.
Overrun by the sound of army tanks heading to war.
I wish I could escape through a door.
Escaping the sounds of gears and ammunition.
But I have to carry on with my country's mission.
It gets me down seeing my friends shot and dead.
I hope I don't take a bullet in the head.
But it's my country's pride that keeps me going
Or even if it isn't showing.
To shed some light on our forgotten past.
Duck and cover here comes the gas.
Like a thick green mist it covers the air.
Lucky enough I'm out of there.
Oh my God the siren is going.
The bomb shelter I better be going.
I could hear the bomb blasts echoing through the ground.
It all stopped not a sound.
We came up quietly, we stood still.
Shocked at the wreckage that lay there.
Does this country really care?
I was so upset that I shed a tear.
Now I will always live in fear.

Clifford Flay (14)

FASHION

F   ashion is different every month
     different styles in and out,

A   lways new shapes and sizes
     sometimes big or even small,

S   ometimes they're striped or maybe patched
     or have fur around the collar and cuffs,

H   eeled boots to small vest tops
     or even mini skirts,

I   n case you didn't know, there are many places
     you can go to get the things you want or need,

O   ne on top of another they go
     into shops like H&M or even Pilot,

N   o one knows what will come next
     into the ever-changing fashion industry.

Emma-Louise Leeming (13)

FRIENDS

Friends are like the sapphire hidden in a
secret place,
So precious.
Life without friends is a life I don't
want to experience.
You never know where you will find a friend.
She may have been your deadliest enemy
Or a boy who is half your age.
Once you've found a special friend
Hold on tight and don't let go
You never know when life will end.

Jodie Crossley

POINTLESS

'What's the point?'
You hear people say.
There is no point
Never, not today.
Blair our Prime Minister
President Bush, USA.
All they do is talk together
Discussing plans every day.
The kind of plans not of how
To make our countries better,
But the ones that are foul.
A killing spread on a letter
The permission to kill:
Innocent and helpless
The elderly and ill
Without remorse, or caring less.
Two men with the power.
Two men with the word.
To start off a great power
That everyone's heard!

Samantha Newman (14)

NASTY GIRL

Lies, pain and deceit
She's full of it from her head to her feet.
She stops at nothing to break people's hearts
Her evilness hits you like a thousand darts.

When she's around she's friendly and lively
But when she's tormenting she's like poison ivy
Yet when it all comes out,
She denies, screams and shouts.

She must be smart, she lies through her teeth,
She must be good because she lies under heat.
She doesn't look guilty, she doesn't give it away,
I promise you this, that one day she'll pay!

Kimberley Elmes (14)

MY GRAN

My gran was so special
She was the head of the pack
She took life as it came
With the good and the bad

My gran was the best
And she never left a mess.
To be with her was like
To be with both of them (Gran and Grandad)

My gran has gone
And it's hard to carry on
But she will always be
Looking after her family.

She was the best
And always will be the best.

Mhairi Stringer (13)

ENTRAPMENT

Northward I stray, within my mind,
I see shadows and despair.
The darkness shows the outline,
Of a long ship waiting there.

The ship that will bear me,
From this heart of odium and fear,
Will bear me to the fair lands,
So far away from here.

Old lands of flowers and lovers,
Sweet lands of hope and grace,
Where waterfalls flow swiftly,
And all are fair of face.

The ship will bear me southwards,
Towards the light side of my mind,
Where all is kind and willing;
The darkness far behind.

But too quickly am I borne,
Towards the east side of my soul,
Where lie my deep ambitions,
Where lies my highest goal.

And here is shown the token,
Reckless hate is ever by,
For here is where it festers,
Not caring if I should die.

And then unto the west side,
Where I seek lands desolate and shoddy,
And here I find my true self,
A child trapped in an adult's body.

Samantha Birch (14)

MY CULTURE

English is our language,
Big breakfasts are our thing!
Football is what we live for,
And to hear our mobiles ring!

We listen to our music,
And drink our English tea.
We love to sing and dance,
While we've got the chance!

We like to party with our friends,
And drive in our Mercedes Benz.
We like to make each other laugh,
When we're feeling down and sad.

Kerry Eccles (13)

BOY!

Boy why do you leave me?
Did I upset you?
Should I have talked more
Or listened harder?

Boy should I have txt more?
We should have met more,
If I had tried harder to talk,
Done more for you,
Make you want me,
Maybe you wouldn't leave.

Maybe is wasn't me
Maybe it's a good thing
Your leaving
But Boy you need to know
I need to tell you this . . .

I love . . .

You!

Natalie Rushton (15)

HOSPITALS

H aving needles in you
O perations you have to have
S preading illnesses
P eople visiting you
I get presents
T he nurses and doctors look after you
A ll mobile phones turned off
L ying in bed all day and all night
S houting and screaming.

Laura Hackney (13)

THE FATHER

His mind as pure as a drop of crystal water,
So straight, like a hawk as it rides through the air.
So strong for the Father is one with the Earth.
That is the Father's mind.

His heart so tender, his words of truth will heal the pain,
That the dear Lord cries for His children to come home.
As a rose that blossoms in a field of flowers,
His love so giving, to embrace people of the world,
He shares the beauty of His love and heart with those of every nation
and country.
That is the Father's heart.

His life so disciplined, for He lives not for Himself,
But for the sake of those around Him.
So much torture, persecution, but He has climbed the mountain,
And flown with the wind, to overcome the black wall of humanity.
He has embraced those who have sought to kill Him.
He has accepted them as His brothers.
He has striven through utter pain -
But has cried many tears of anguish only for the children of God.
To renew the leaves on the big oak tree,
To restore the pieces of the puzzle from this fallen world.
He holds his hands high upon the translucent sky,
With righteousness and power.
This is the Father's life.

My eyes fill with tears, for words cannot describe
How much He sacrifices for the sake of the cosmos.
He will stand until the end, and shall not tire,
The one absolute Father!
The Father of true love!
He is the all-giving and all-living.
He is the true Father.

Rosanna O'Connell (13)

THE BATTLE OF HASTINGS

At the start of the Battle Of Hastings,
Harold and William prepared,
For the contest between the two,
But neither of them seemed scared.

At the bottom of Senlac Hill,
The Normans stood side by side,
A trumpet sounded, a cheer went up,
They moved forward like a rushing tide.

The Saxons did not move, their shields out in front,
They were a fearless army with confidence in their eyes,
But the Normans stopped, arrows flew from their bows,
The Saxons looked up as darkness filled the sky.

The devious Normans thought of a plan,
They ran up the hill looking brave,
Then they retreated back down again,
And the Saxons followed in a wave.

It was the end of the Saxon army,
Harold got an arrow in his eye,
William had won this terrific day,
And Harold king of the Saxons was left
                          on the field to die.

William, Duke Of Normandy,
Had beat his Saxon rivals,
The Normans still stood strong,
Just as they did on their arrival.

Nicky Johnson

THE FIELD

So quiet now, except the distant sonnet of a single bird; so far away,
And the desperate flapping of cloth on the wire,
Like a scarf of an old lady at a train station as the 14.52 rattles past -
so far away,
Still the rag flaps - echoing in the vast grey openness.

Once a beautiful golden field of sun grew here,
Now there is nothing but a brown ocean - littered with the lives
of too many men;
Their once smart, shining, stately uniforms
Are now dank grey, torn rags stained with blood - so thick,
so dark, so pure
So young.

Billy Davis lies face down in the mud - he drowned in the brown hell,
His leg is six feet above his matted black hair -
entangled in barbed wire.
It starts to rain - the water tries to wash away the sin that was here,
To wash away the blood and the mud, to erase the
monstrosities witnessed.
A droplet forms on the tip of Billy's finger - still warm.

At the top of the mound, a lone poppy stands triumphant,
Overseeing operations on the devil's construction site.
He bows his head in respect - the only life left weeps
at what it has seen.

A private sits huddled in a puddle at the bottom of his bunker.
His face so white, so petrified - so young.
His hand trembles in his lap, his eyes fixated
on his brother in front of him - so cold.
It could have been him . . . but it wasn't.
And now he sits huddled and dying in a place a million times crueller,
colder, further away from life than hell could ever be.

So quiet now, except the distant sound of a real man; crying.

Martin Dorset-Purkis (15)

THE VICTIM'S THOUGHTS

Inside I'm like a raging sea,
I only got called one name,
But it meant so much to me,
I tried to laugh it off at first,
Then I saw the hand drawing closer,
Wham it hit me around my face,
Don't say anything,
She'll just think I'm a baby,
I just walk away,
I wonder if it will happen again,
Maybe then I will tell someone,
I couldn't say anything this time
It might have only been an accident.
She says sorry,
She doesn't mean it though.
It's just a way of making her look innocent.
The bully won again.

Emily Elson (13)

ONE HURT, NO PAIN

The amount of times I've forgiven her,
The things she does,
It hurts so much,
Like I'm being stabbed in the back,
Continuously.

Then there's him,
He knows how I feel,
The thing he did,
That hurts so much more,
Every time I walk past,
Just glance at him,
It feels like my heart
Is being wrenched out of my chest,
But it's also tight,
So tight I can hardly breathe.

I felt that once before,
But before there was no other pain,
That pain was heart-wrenching,
Almost painless but now it's not like that,
I wonder if it'll ever go back to the way it was before.
One hurt,
No pain.

Makeeta Pooley (15)

LARA AND TED

There were two crooks called Lara and Ted;
Who had to steal for their daily bread.

Lara and Ted went to the shop;
They stole some sweets and a pork chop.

They went to the bakers to steal some bread;
As they walked in Lara banged her head.

One afternoon the shop had to close;
As Ted climbed in, he cut his nose.

A fruit shop opened down the road;
Ted and Lara stole a load.

They stole for days, even weeks;
They also decided to steal some leeks.

One day they had a great thought;
But they didn't know they would get caught.

They never knew they would do the time;
Although they did a terrible crime.

And now the moral, crime never pays;
You'd best take note of this worthy phrase.

But now their bodies are underground,
Left to rot until they're found.

Lauren Warne (13)

THE MONSTROUS TEEN

It all started when Mum said,
'Tidy your room!'

A thump on the stairs,
A slam of a door.
I grab all my books,
Throw them on to the floor.

The music goes on,
I want to destroy!
My dad comes up,
'What's that noise?'

Now I'm in a mood,
Mum's shouting at me.
My sister laughs,
'You're acting like you're three!'

Then all goes quiet,
There's no noise anywhere.
I decide to say sorry,
Until next time, to my lair!

Javneet Ghuman (13)

TEENAGE WORRIES

Clean your room!
Tidy your bed!
Those are the words that run through my head.
Day in, day out
Those are the words that Mum always shouts.

I go up in my room and escape from all the noise.
Instead this is my space.
My space where nobody can shout at me.
This is my own very special place.

Olivia O'Sullivan (13)

FRIENDSHIP IS . . .

Friendship is a shoulder to cry on
Friendship is a mop for the tears that fall
Friendship is a clown full of smiles
Friendship is a lifetime full of laughs
Friendship is . . .

Friendship is a roller coaster of emotions
Friendship is a healer of broken hearts
Friendship is a shower of love
Friendship is a priceless love
Friendship is . . .

Gemma Wright (13)

DEATH

Death,
Overcoming like a dark shadow,
Death,
Like a stranger dragging you into the unknown.

Death,
A black coat hugging, pulling at you,
To come,
Hard to stay warm without it.

Death,
A black hand blocking out the sunlight,
Forever,
And turning down the volume,
Until you are gone.

Death,
Nothing more to say.

Lucy Elliott (13)

DREAMS COME TRUE

My dream come true, is to be a model,
When I'm older.
My dream come true, is to be a film star,
When I'm older.
My dream come true, is to be an artist,
At all times.
My dream come true, is to be whatever I
Want to be.

Laila Innes (14)

TEENAGERS

Every teenager
Has a life of their own.
That leads to the future
In one way or more.

All of us are different,
From fashion
To passion.
Who do you admire?

Charlotte Turner (13)

WHAT IS A TEENAGER?

What is a teenager?
I ask this question here.
What is a teenager?
Adulthood is near.
What is a teenager?
Baggy shirts and jeans.
What is a teenager?
Against the wall it leans.
What is a teenager?
Someone without a care?
What is a teenager?
Crazy music and crazy hair.
What is a teenager?
A fun-filled life it leads.
What is a teenager?
To be noticed it pleads.

A teenager's world is full of tests,
Full of pranks and full of jests.
A teenager may be a funny creature,
But you've got to be mad to be its teacher.

Charlie Baxter (13)

YOU ARE THE ONE
(Dedicated to my wonderful mum)

You are the one I dream about all night and all day,
You are the one I never want to ever go away.
You are the one who wonders at the midnight sky,
You are the one admiring all the different birds that fly.
You are the one who wipes the teardrops from my cheek,
You are the one afraid of snow on a mountain peak.
You are the one arranging all the gorgeous flowers,
You are the one who speeds up all those long and boring hours.
You are the one who saved me from my traumatic past,
You are the one to whom I give love that I truly want to last.

Helen Russell

LATE NIGHT PUNISHMENT

Monday night,
It's half-past seven,
Out with my mates,
Till almost eleven.

I get back home,
Mum says, 'Where've you been?
I've been worried sick,
You're only thirteen!'

I turn away,
And walk up the stairs.
'It's school tomorrow!'
As if I care!

I walk into my room,
Slam the door shut,
Mum can be really annoying,
You should have seen that look!

At least she stopped yapping,
I can get to bed,
But I keep hearing her,
Over and over in my head.

I know she doesn't mean to,
She does it 'cause she cares.
It's good to have a mum,
A mum who's always there.

Laura Southcott (13)

WHY IS IT?

Why are we put on this Earth?
Is it to live?
Is it to hurt?
Is it to die?
Why let people run your life,
Just because they're bigger than you?
Just because they're much more overpowering than you?
What's the point in trying to be heard?
A bully will just come back again,
A bully will make sure you're shamed.
Why me?
  Why?
    Why?
      Why?

Colton Killingback

LIFE

Life's a journey everyone must make,
The roads are winding, but one you must take.
Whether it leads to good or bad, is up to you,
But no matter what, believe and you will pull through.

Life's a journey everyone must make,
The boats are speeding, so follow their wake.
It may lead to something new
But whatever you choose, it's up to you.

So follow your heart, before it's too late
Because the train is leaving and it won't wait.

Jaimee Le Resche (14)

ODE TO DOUBLE GEOGRAPHY

Plunged into the depths of darkness,
Oblivion, hell and fire,
We fall, slowly suffocated by our screams,
Living death floating past our weary eyes.
Dull and drear, shrouds us like a cloak of doom.
Surrounding us with fear,
The light has drowned,
Here, like corpses
Deflated, we lie.

Candice Parfitt (13)

DREAMS

Little girl dreams
Of fairy princes
And golden castles
And kings and queens.

We're not allowed to dream,
Not any more.
We're the top set, the stressed set.
Eleven GCSEs - all A to C.

We're still just kids
Expected to act like adults,
Having to see the world as it is,
Face reality far too soon.

Helen Ewen (14)

THE OLD MAN IN MY HOUSE

There was an old man
Who used to live in my house
He lived all alone
Apart from one mouse.

But he is still here,
I saw him one night
I jumped straight out of bed
I had such a fright.

He was in my doorway,
Standing, watching me
And I saw just below him
That a dog was at his knee.

He whistles in the kitchen,
He hums as he walks up the stairs
He strolls along the hallways
He appears to have no cares.

He sits in his chair in the living room
Reading a see-through book
He scares me because he's a ghost,
But he has a kind and gentle look.

To everyone else, he's invisible,
Nobody can hear him speak,
It's as if he never existed
Though his past may have been quite bleak.

There is an old man
Who lives in my house
No one else notices him
He's as quiet as a mouse.

Emma Phillips (13)

STOP THE FIGHTING, STOP THE KILLING, STOP THE WAR

Is war the answer?
World War I and II, Pearl Harbour
September 11th.
Tragic events, but was there really victory -
Is fighting back the answer?

Declaring war after such events,
Bombing countries, killing innocent souls
Make us just as bad as they are.
What pleasure can you get out of
Killing innocent people, innocent children?
Revenge is always sweet, but it can leave
A bitter taste in your mouth.
So is it worth it?

Anger fills up inside you,
You want to do to them, what they have done to you!
But is war the answer?
I dream of world peace, people living in harmony
No fighting, no killing, no war
But this seems impossible.
War outlives us all.

Surely there is more to the world than war -
But we can't see it because war is in the way?
There won't be a world left for your
Children or children's children.
So stop the fighting. Stop the killing. Stop the war.

Emma Collins (15)

MY HOMELAND IS . . . HM . . .

Living far away, from your loved ones,
feeling alone at night.
Wondering what they are up to
in my long lost, unknown homeland.

Where do I come from? They apply
Who am I? I ask.
That five letter question can unlock
me deeply, deeply into my past.
Most important, deeply to my curiosity.

Is my homeland far?
Maybe that's why it brings racism so near!

The difference in food,
The comparison between languages,
The variety in taste,
The contrast in culture.

Are these all major issues?
Well, it doesn't matter anymore,
because now I can say
bravely and loudly . . .
My homeland is China!

Linh Dieu (14)

WHAT COULD I KNOW?

It's just hormones they say
And they're probably right
You're just a dumb kid
An insult to sight

What could you know?
Well I'll tell you, I say
I know of deadlines
I know of delay

I know of fearing
And also fun too
I know of laughter
I know how to be true

I know of embarrassment
I know of disgrace
I know of failure
And hiding my face

I know of beauty
And also of hope
I know of stupidity
I know how to cope

I know how to live
In the world all around
I know where buses
And trains can be found

In one brief summation
Of what I know to be true
I'm definitely sure
That I know more than you.

Orlando de Lange (14)

WHAT NOW?

All this pressure is put upon me,
What else do they expect me to be?
My parents want one thing, my teacher's another.
For my friends, something else. Why do I bother?
All I do is never enough.
All this judgement, don't they know they're being a bit rough?
Changing myself to be what they want me to be -
Aren't I good enough, just being me?
Well today I have decided, no longer will I change,
I don't care what they think, I will not rearrange!

Rebecca Cunningham (15)

TRAPPED

I was inside a room
There were four walls,
I was trying to escape through the door,
But it was impossible.
It was like it was solid.
I began drowning -
Not with water, but with problems.
I had no way of getting out.
What could I do?
No one to turn to!
I began to talk to myself out loud,
Dealing with them,
Not letting them eat me up any more.
Then the problems disappeared,
The door opened and I became free.
I began to get more confident,
I could enjoy myself again.
No more crying at night or when alone,
Whilst dealing with them in privacy, as best I could,
But being free, forever.

Zara Flight (13)

ME, AT THE AGE OF 14

14 the year of stress
14 the year of coursework
14 of the year of conflict with parents
14 the year of studying
14 the year of spending parent's money!
14 the year of getting what you want
14 the year of ringing friends
14 the year of always shouting!
14 the year of fighting with my big sister
14 the year of going out
14 the year of wanting what you can't have
14 the year of feeling alone
14 the year of change.

Kerrie Cooke (14)

MY MOTHER

A distance not far behind
Remember the signs?
I counted them, one by one.
Sadness wasn't so far ahead
Remember the words whispered?
I sang them to you,
Like children we sat.
Remember the games?
I remember when you held my hand
Remember that?
I smile when I think of it,
Where did you go?
Why did you go?
Remember me?
My old friend
Remember the tears cried?
I cried upon your shoulder
So many times.
How are you - do you exist anymore?
My invisible friend.

Rosie Wilkes (14)

SEND ME THERE

Life to life
and mind to mind
my spirit now
will intertwine
I meld my soul
and journey too
the ones whose thoughts
I wish I knew

Heaven to Hell
and death to death
send me there
till I pass the test
to become the best
and beat the rest.

Kerry Weston (14)

CONFUSED?

Help! I'm confused, so . . .
I sit myself down and ask myself a question
Who am I?
Am I nice or mean -
Am I lazy or keen?
Help! I don't know who I am!

Help! I'm confused, so . . .
I sit myself down and ask myself a question
What do I want to do?
Be a musician or a writer -
Be a teacher or a rights fighter?
Help! I don't know what to do!

Help! I'm confused, so . . .
I sit myself down and ask myself a question
Who should I listen to?
My friends or my family -
My teachers or the man on the telly?
Help! I don't know who to listen to!

I'm confused, so . . .
I sit myself down and ask myself a question
What will my future be like?
Will there be war or peace -
Will the pollution cease?
Help! What will my future be like?

Abigail Higson (13)

ALONE

Who loves a teenager?
Who wants a teenager?
Who wants our mood swings?
Who knows us?

Are we alone?
Do we feel alone?
Or do we just feel alone?
Are there other teenagers alone?

Are we wanted?
Do we feel wanted?
Is love wanted?
Who or what can answer our wants?

Can we love?
Are we loveable?
Do we want to be loved?
Do we feel loved?

Marc Cochrane (15)

DREAMING

Someone, somewhere
Dreams of your smile
And whilst thinking of you
Says life is worthwhile.
So when you feel lonely
Remember it's true
Somebody, somewhere
Is dreaming of you!

Rachel Cork (14)

THE SPLIT

You hide in a room,
Where you think you're safe.
Words sail through walls
Full of anger and hate.

You feel the cracks appearing,
You see your world split.
Confusion fills your wounds
Your gashes seem to grow.

Clouds are all you see,
Above the thick fog,
Blackness is your outlook
You're searching for the light.

Sarah Edwards (15)

IF ONLY HE KNEW

I saw him standing across the road, looking so divine,
My heart started pounding like mad, as if it was a sign.
I stood across from him, staring as if I was in a trance,
He looked over and waved, followed by a quick, sweet glance.
If only he knew how I felt, then maybe things would change,
Maybe he would understand why I always act so strange.
I act differently when he's around, I act really weird and funny,
He's standing across the road, with no idea that he's my honey.
I think he only sees me as a friend, someone to rely on -
Someone to go to when he's in trouble, a shoulder to cry on.
I wish he felt the same way, it would be a dream come true,
We would be together forever, each day through and through.

Every night when I lie in bed, I see his beautiful face,
In my dreams I am his bride, wearing a dress of white satin and lace.
Hopefully one day we will be together and be madly in love,
And when we are in Heaven, he will be my sweet, white dove.

Lyndi McDougall (14)

AMAZING GRACE

Bursting through the door,
I rush along the floor
And peep into the cot,
I see a tiny tot.
Grace.

She's only four hours old
And has already put our lives on hold.
When I saw her, my heart skipped a beat,
I'd never seen such a beautiful girl.
Grace.

She opens her eyes and pools of blue look up at me,
As if she knew,
It was me.
Her lips are a bloomed rose waiting to be kissed.
Grace.

I take her hand,
She grabs my finger
And I stand quite still content to linger.
I look at her mum, exhausted yet pleased.
I look at her dad who won't stop grinning.
They both nod.
Yes, I pick her up and hold her close to me,
Her sweet breath covers my face.
Amazing Grace.

Eleanor Riley (13)

LIFE AS A SPECIALLY-BRED MAGGOT

Just lying here
Without a body yet,
Plenty of time to stand and stare,
If only I had a pair of eyes so that I could!

Finally, the time has come,
As I emerge from my womb as such.
I feel the urge to have a fat munch.
I am here all alone, unable to communicate,
Yet surrounded by others in the same situation.
Some green, some red, some blue, some just like me,
Whatever colour that is!
I cannot tell, for I have no eyes.

As I get plumper
All the others get taken away,
Only to be replaced by more,
I now have a terrible weight on my shoulders.
Literally, if I had any -
I am now seeing life as a food user and nothing else,
For I am frail, and have no bones,
Soon my time will come.

I get older and waste away,
Hurrah! My time has come.
In a pot I go, how long passes I don't know!
And then I feel a prick, a hook is in me.
I squirm for a while, until I'm drowned
And now I'm dead.

I'm writing to you from maggot heaven,
I've just found out I was only the lava of a fly,
And this was a mere fraction of my life.

Alastair Band (13)

OTHERS

When I stare in your eyes
I think of a blue night sky,
And the tap, tap, tap in my mind
Portrays the kind.
As I open the doors
To your heart
I can't part.
My hands are stuck to yours
But laws
Keep us apart.
For a second I dart,
When I realise the dark
Makes a mark
Upon my skin.

Fern Shepherd (15)

THE REAL ME

Please don't judge me by my face,
My religion or my race.
Please don't laugh at what I wear,
Or how I act or do my hair.
Just look a little deeper,
Way down, deep inside.
And although you might not see it,
I have a lot to hide.
Behind my dark clothes is
Where my secrets lie,
Behind my smile, I softly cry.
People stare but they can't see
All my thoughts that live inside me.
If you look closer you would find
A lonely little girl, who shares my mind.
Please just get to know her
And maybe you will see
That if you look deep enough,
You will find the real me.

Rachael Mueller (14)

ALONE

The sun is one of its kind
When the moon swallows it up, it doesn't seem to mind.
The golden coin spinning in the sky,
Even the moon has the stars for company, way up high.
But the sun is alone,
It doesn't have a mouth to moan.

The lone oak tree, standing there,
The harsh wind stripping it bare
Of its companions - the leaves.
A mighty sigh of lonesomeness it heaves,
It's a horrible thing, being alone,
It doesn't have the ability of speech, so it can't moan.

The stray dog abandoned and despised,
The lonesome loneliness it has to bide.
All alone in the dank and dark,
No one will talk to him, from human to lark.
The poor dog, it didn't choose to be alone.
No one will listen to its whine or moan.

If everyone had someone, it wouldn't be so bad,
If everyone had someone, it wouldn't be so sad.

Zippy Jason (13)

DOESN'T IT DRIVE YOU MAD?

Doesn't it drive you mad,
The way teachers go on and on
About your homework?

Doesn't it drive you mad,
The way parents tell you to be polite
And do what you're told?

I just want to be rude
And do what I want!
Oh, doesn't it drive you mad?

Anna Harper (15)

MONEY

Have you ever noticed
When you want something
You never have any money?

But when you do have money
It seems like you have loads of it
The world is yours
And you can buy anything you want?

The smell
The feel
It's money
Everyone adores it.

The way it looks
You admire it
You stare at all the notes
And the Queen stares back at you.

It's the best feeling in the world.

Then you realise
That what you bought
Isn't what you thought you bought!

What you had
Was a waste of money
But you can't take it back now
You've used it.

All that precious money wasted,
Just like that!
Never to be seen again.
Well not until next pocket-money day!

Jessica Debnam (13)

STAR FRIEND

How lonely it can be, surrounded by a crowd,
I try to keep my distance, in the corner, my head's bowed.
I live a life of silence, a silence that seems to have no end.
A silence that can be shattered by no one, not even a close friend.
At night I thank God for the blessings that I gain,
For the times that I am happy, the times I have no pain.
When the time comes, when sadness fills my heart,
It's always best to tell my fears, to the nearest star.

Melissa McCarroll (14)

SNOW

When the snow will fall
Then the children will show
The snowball fights will begin
And sledge rides
Down the hill
Children become happy
Smiles shine through
All is white
Crisp and new
Best news they say
There's no school today!

Barry Alker (15)

FRIENDSHIP

Friends can drive you round the bend
Only because they're a sensitive friend.
Friends can sometimes make you sad
Sometimes they can make you glad

Friends come in all sizes and shapes
Some dressed in hats, gloves and capes.
Friends can be skinny and tall
Some can be fat and small

Friends can be very caring
They can sometimes be very daring,
Friends can drive you round the bend
Only because they're an emotional friend

Some friends are soft 'n' gentle
But my friends are marvellously mental
Friends should be happy and free
Just like you and me!

Priya Kaur (13)

FOOTBALL MAD

Football crazy
Football mad
Leicester scored a goal
And everyone went mad

Leicester 1-0
That's not bad
But come on, we need more
So score, score, score

We can do it
We can win
Can Elliott score this one?
Yes! It's in

It's 2-0 to Leicester
A very good score
But now there's a sheep on the pitch
Going baa, baa, baa

The sheep is now off
And the match carries on
We can continue
And make the other team go wrong

It is half-time
But the match may be off
It's raining so hard
And the pitch is waterlogged

The match is abandoned
It's so unfair
We were winning
And doing so well

So we'll have to play
them again then, won't we?

Daniel Paget (13)

PROBLEMS OF A TEEN

In your teenage years
You don't know what to do
Your feelings are all mixed up
You haven't got a clue

You are too young for pubs
And too old for toys
The only thing interesting
Are the teenage boys

Your hormones are flying everywhere
Fall outs with your friends
Trying to do well at school
And keeping up with trends

Every day you are fighting
Each and every spot
Then you start to worry
When you get a lot

But there are upsides
To growing up
As long as you are happy
And don't care how you look.

Rachael Wagstaff (13)

DESIGNER LABEL

Everyone thinks I'm one of their gang
Wear their fashion
Speak their slang
But I change my look every day
Don't judge me . . . not fickle
It's just a game to play

On Monday, a schoolgirl
Start the week neat
Tie right, shirt right
Homework complete

Tuesday, Military Miss
In green and brown
Camouflage and combats
As I walk round town

Wednesday, it's punk
Blacks and reds
Partying in my fishnets
Hair in dreads

Thursday, I'm sporty
Grey, pink, Lonsdale too
Friday, I'm a skater
Hoodies in baby blue

Saturday, boho babe
Cords and purple tops
Suede handbag, far too small
When I hit the shops

Sunday, I'm whatever I want to be
I'm a little preppy, sporty, funky, punky, skater Barbie
And I'm happy . . . so . . .

Label me.

Emma Leedham (15)

It's A Free Country - Right?

Not if you sleep in a doorway
With your feet always cold.
Not when police shift you in the morning,
And you hate to do as you're told.

Not when you have to beg
And only get a few pounds.
Not when you smell really bad,
So bad you get chased by hounds.

Not if people just ignore you,
Pretend you don't exist.
Not when you can't get a job,
And there is nothing you can do.

Not when people nick your stuff,
And you can't fight back.
Not when you can't change your clothes,
You feel you should be dead.

John MacColl

GROWING UP

I have been born,
I've took my first step,
I've said my first word,
I've took my time growing up
And I've left school.
The problem is what do I do now?
Nowhere to stay
Nowhere to eat
And nowhere to sleep.
I feel I have taken a bigger step in life,
Now I need to look after myself,
Start as poor
Finish as rich.
It will take time for me to grow into
The world but it will be worth it.

David Caswell (13)

IS IT LOVE?

Embracing your body
Holding you near
The way that you touch me
Excludes me from fear.

As blue as the ocean
As clear as the skies
I feel such emotion
When I drown in your eyes.

Kissing you softly
Brushing your skin
I can't help this feeling
It lives deep within.

Cry when you leave me
Heart breaks in two
I don't know how to say it
But I guess
I love you.

Bethany Edwards (15)

SILENCE

The sound is silent
She says nothing,
You don't understand her,
But you don't need to.

Her face gives a misunderstood impression,
A dark cloud of despair.

She is alone.

There is nothing, all is dead,
She says nothing when she wakes up from her bed.

She is alone.

She glides from person to person,
Not a word is spoken.

Some people say she doesn't care!

Then why is she really there?

Questions are asked but deserve no reply.

She is silent!

Why?

Elysia Clarke (15)

NIGHT

Night is black
Like a raven's wing
Speckled with
Shining stars
It flows like black
Ink from a quill
And envelops
Everything in
Its path
Its cover hides
Creatures of
The dark,
Who howl
Scratch and bite,
Anyone who
May enter their
Dark and
Bleak world.

Kristel Wan (13)

TEENAGERS!

We leave our rooms untidy,
We leave the bathroom a mess.
We try and dodge our homework.
We never revise for tests.

We borrow money off our parents.
Go to the cinema with our friends.
We watch TV till midnight.
Drive our parents round the bend.

'Why?' is parents often asked question?
And here's the answer too,
'Because' is our favourite phrase,
We're teenagers and it's what we *do!*

Fiona Maguire (13)

THAT BOY

He's kind, he's polite,
he's cute but shy.
What am I going to do, it's the boy I like?

His hair is black,
he gels it back.
He's tall but thin
he's the real thing.

He plays football like nobody does
that's why everybody calls him Buff.

My heart is thumping
my friends are jumping.
Oh my God, he's coming over!

Nuray Vardan (13)

A Walk In The Park

As the sun shines and the heat comes down,
The park is minutes away from the local town.

Sitting on a swing, going to and fro,
A friend comes to say, 'Hello!'

I was thinking about my dream,
She was thinking about strawberries and cream.

I got off the swing and walked across the wooded bark,
I said to her, 'With your boyfriend, is there still that spark?'

I said to her, 'I fancy somebody, loads!'
I looked at my watch and realised I was late.

Along the firm, clean, green grass
We took, the park pass.
We stopped off at Nina's house
She said goodbye, as she went into see her pet mouse.

I went and had tea
I was meeting my dream, in secrecy.

As I walked back over the moonlit park,
I thought, *now this is my turn to spark.*

There he was, waiting for me
His face was a big glee.

He kissed me on the cheek
I thought I'd better speak.

As we walked to the bench, hand in hand,
Our shadows on the floor made by the moon, did expand.

Emily Bower (14)

ZITS

It screams to be squeezed, the temptation
it's hard to bear.
It grows and grows, like it's gonna explode.
I think it will never stop,
I cover it with make-up, thick, like plastercast,
now everybody's looking at my silly mask.
Boys don't want to know me,
my friends take the mick.
And all because of this, humongous zit.
The pressure's getting harder,
it's sore to the touch.
Then all of a sudden
Pop!
Aggh!

Jade Sade Mayers (14)

THE OTHER SIDE OF MYSELF

The souls of the damned have taken my heart.
It has been ripped from me by their murderous hands.
My pain is eternal; I can't forgive nor forget,
No one can understand, the hate that I feel.

The people who did this, the b******s are scum,
They are lower than dirt, lower than all things which creep and crawl.
They are not worth the dust that the angry wind blows in their faces,
They are not worth a tenth of my lost love.

The fires of my eyes burn with the lust for revenge,
I need to see pain; I need to see rivers run red with their blood.
I'll twist with my knife, cut, hack, slash and wreak havoc.
One day I'll draw, with these hands, my heart's name on their
unrecognisable faces.

I shall enjoy this revenge; I care not if my life ends
on this moonlit night.
The fury of the ages flows through my veins.
The hot bubbling anger makes my blood boil as if
all past cases of injustice must be solved through me.

If this vengeance is not mine, I pray that the shades of misery and death
cut them down and pull them apart, one by one.
Until the dust settles and my prey have gone.

Bethany Mead (15)

Science: Beautiful, Dangerous, Liberating

The Aurora Borealis electrons gather and make it shine,
A honeycomb fitted together with all its glory,
Computers, industrialise the way we live,
Cars work by smart cards,
The Japanese attacking America in WWII using the jet stream,
The atomic bomb on Hiroshima
Anthrax poisoning the way we life.

Ben Charlton (13)

DESPAIRING DESPERATION

As she stares through the streets
And down at her feet,
She cries for her love
She sees the dream of a dove.

She prays for forgiveness,
She begs for a light
Her fingers are busy
Her mind dazed by her plight.

The terror of night comes all too soon,
The sun's hope is swallowed, replaced by the moon.
The stars twinkle out, a false comfort light,
The crescent moon shivers and fills her with fright.

As the sparkling diamonds shine through the dark,
She hears the last nightingale, and prays for a lark.
As she silently screams for her first love she sighs,
The night stays quiet, as silent as mice.
Does any wind howl? No, there is none.
And bitterest anger gloats that he's won.

The darkness hovers for longer each night,
Until eventually it never gives way to the light.
The rope hangs before her, now covered with dew,
As she sighs once again and cries tears anew.
She climbs the strong tree, the noose in her hand,
And takes a last look at the mortal land.

The loop round her neck, she closes her eyes,
She jumps from the branch, through the air she flies.
As her neck breaks, her soul carries on,
The body stays swinging, for hatred has won.

Joanna Taylor (14)

EXPLANATION

Although we slam doors, shout, be stubborn and scream,
Although we always seem to need new tops and jeans,
Although we play heavy metal rock, loudly until three,
This is the way we live our life, it's just meant to be.

Although we are always handing in our homework two days late,
Although we gossip through your lessons about last night's hot date,
Although we disagree with you when you tell us to act more mature,
You must understand we can't, cos then life would be such a bore.

Although we call you names like 'retard' and 'baboon'
Although we always tell on you, when you sneak into our room,
Although we always pick fights with you for no apparent reason at all,
It's our job to torment you younger siblings, from the moment you
learn to crawl

Although we always look suspicious when we walk round the shops,
Although we seem to get our kicks out of pranks calling the cops,
Although we get rowdy and occasionally trash the school bus,
We're just misunderstood individuals,
What would the world be without us?

Harriet Hayter (13)

DISCOVERY

He was there when they discovered it,
That tiny metal cocoon,
He was there when they discovered it
Sitting in that room.

Little did he know when they discovered it,
The terror it would bring.
Little did they know when they discovered it,
That it was such an evil thing.

For when they discovered it,
It was all that is evil and sad.
Yet he rejoiced when they discovered it
He believes good comes from bad.

The end they saw when they discovered it,
The end in that strange cocoon,
The beginning he saw when they discovered it,
A beginning of suffering and doom.

The world did not know when they discovered it,
All the screams, terror and pain,
But he knew when they discovered it,
Things would never be the same.

It has been lost since they discovered it,
But it will soon be found,
And when they rediscover it,
There will be that fearful sound.

And when they rediscover it,
His efforts will not have been in vain,
For when they rediscover it,
It will be Death's greatest reign.

Ella Woodbridge (15)

IMAGINE

Imagine you're a sports star
competing with the rest.

Imagine you're a genius
inventing all the best.

Imagine you are popular
mingling with the stars.

Imagine that you're rich,
driving expensive cars.

I imagine all of this,
which races my heartbeat.

I want all my dreams to come true,
to make my life complete.

Jason Barnes (15)

HE HAD A DREAM

An insignificant child in a crazy world,
One small person, known only by a few,
Slowly growing, slowly learning,
The impact on the world this child will have,
If they only knew.

This child will grow, this child will learn,
This child will also weep,
But in the end this child will be,
Known for his courage so deep.

No one knew what this child could do,
No one thought there was a way,
No one believed he could make a difference,
Until that beautiful day.

His speech is renowned all over the world,
He's praised for his eternal hope,
He will never be forgotten for what he did,
Meaning that his people didn't just have to cope.

Helen Proffitt (13)

PEOPLE DON'T THINK

People don't think I care
People don't think I get scared.
People don't think I worry
People don't think that I hurry.
They just think I'm there
Empty and boring.

I care about boyfriends
I get scared at scary films.
I worry when I've got a spot
I'm in a hurry when I'm late to see my friends
Seeming like I don't care.
But I'm not like that -
Although everyone thinks I am.

People don't think I struggle
People don't think I have a heart.
People don't think I'm lonely
People don't think I think
They don't think I feel.

I struggle at decisions
Somewhere there's a heart but it's hidden deep.
I get lonely when people are cruel
I think about the world
About the grass and the trees
And the flowers and the sun . . . and life.

People don't understand me
So they turn away.
They don't think I get hurt
They think I'm strong, so they just stand and stare.

I dream about small things which matter to me,
They don't know me, not at all.

Carrie Pitt (15)

THIS IS THE GREED OF MEN

The hour will come
When the last lion
Is hunted and slain.
The world will continue
Selfish for power.
This is the greed of men
Just the hunter shrugs,
'What next, I wonder?' He asks
And he moves on.
He doesn't care
Doesn't care he has
Destroyed the last king.
This is the greed of men,
When the last war is fought,
Over the last of the land.
This is the greed of men.
The sun still shines down
Through a gaping
Hole in the atmosphere.
Now throw the last spear,
The last man falls.
The moon beams on,
Silver over slaughter.
He has never seen this before,
For this is the greed of men
This is total annihilation!

Harriet Drouin (14)

QUE SERA, SERA

What will tomorrow bring?
What does my future involve?
Will it be hard and trying
Or will it be easy and boring?

Will I be happy and contented
Or will I be sad and heart rented?
Will my life be rose-scented
Or will my pride be ever dented?

All these questions keep racking my brain,
If I carry on like this, I'll be going insane.
My life may be hellishly hard,
Or it may be boringly easy.

As an answer to these questions, people say to me,
'Que sera, sera!'
What will be, will be.

Louis Ashburner (14)

THE CASTLE

The castle has been deserted for decades
Now it stands alone on the cliffs
It looks dull but when the sun shines
It sparkles like a gift from God

If you stand within its walls
And stare at the outside world
You can see the ocean stretch out
An endless blue carpet

The sounds inside are few and quiet
The chirping of birds, the swaying of trees
Time appears to be moving in slow motion
A second feels like an hour

Its walls have crumbled over time
Making it look ragged and weak
But its presence is still mysterious
As it looks out across the lands.

Craig Brusby (13)

AALIYAH

Born a princess
Died an angel
On Earth she lived for twenty years

Aaliyah's life had only just begun
Her voice was beautiful
Like her sun-kissed skin

Aaliyah's career may have been short
But she is still an inspiration.
I can understand why, God
Would want you close to him

You were truly an angel on Earth
You'll always be remembered
Rest in peace, baby girl.

Karen Kontoh (16)

AUTUMN'S SONG

The autumn's song is a beautiful thing,
If you listen carefully, you can hear
birds as they sing.
I wonder what next autumn will bring -
Will it be the same?
Will leaves fall off the trees?

In summer I wonder how much
honey we can get from the bees,
All of this to hear autumn's song,
I know autumn is nice, but I hope
it won't stay long.
I hope summer will come and
Autumn will go.
Oh don't the seasons move
ever so slow.
Just to hear autumn's song

Daniel Foster (15)

WAR

Ever since that day in September,
Which people will always remember,
We've been told to prepare for war.

So everything has been put on hold
Until we have been told
When the war has started.

Now we have to wait and see,
What the answer is to be -
Are we going to war?

Out there already are Britain and the USA
Germany and France may
But are we going to attack?

Is this going to be
World War III,
Only time will tell.

Jonathan Chinnock (13)

SEEING STARS

U2 round the corner
Beethoven up a tree,
Abba at the cinemas
And oh look, it's Queen.

Mum's been seeing Beatles
Climbing over our wall,
Dad's positive it's Shania Twain
That's mowing the lawn.
My brother has seen Boyzone
Playing in the park,
And sis has noticed Spice Girls
Walking in the dark.
Gran says that she saw Elvis
Just the other day,
While Grandpa knows it was Phil Collins
On the motorway.

Now this must sound quite crazy
But it's that lot who are weird,
There's no need to tell me
I know I'm Britney Spears!

Emma Pettet (14)

THE LESSON OF WAR

We both received a letter this morning,
that is, my brother and I.
One asking me to write a poem,
the other asking him to die.

He thinks it's brave to fight for your country,
and this world full of hatred and lies.
As a tear rolls down my face,
more innocent people die.

Why go to war with each other,
and ruin this beautiful world we have?
People like me care for one another,
will their lives always be this bad?

So here's a lesson for Blair,
and of course Saddam Hussein!
Say goodbye to your freedom,
'cause like my brother, you won't see it again.

Hannah Smith (13)

LIFE AS A TEEN

Life as a teen,
Can be mean,
I don't want to grow old,
Nor do I want to go bald.

I loved my childhood,
I still want to listen about Little Red Riding Hood,
But how can I?
If time flies.

I want to enjoy life,
With friends and family,
So I guess every second counts,
As time mounts,
Tonight I'm going to make it right,
By doing the best in life and make it an example,
For the people of the world.

Shabrina Ali (13)

WITCHES' CAULDRON RECIPE

Wing of a bat, one hair of Hecate,
The horn of a devil, cold scrapings from a plate.
Tail of a dog, the elbow of a child,
The roar of a lion, straight from the wild.
A stormy cloud, the screech of crows,
Hairy wart from an old man's nose.
An egg gone bad, a sock with mould,
A spider's web, glistening in the cold.

Stir it up and make it thick,
Drink it up to make you sick.

Whisker of a kitten, the eyes of a wren,
Darkest secrets of a thousand men.
Squeak of a mouse, the sting of a bee,
Broken shells, from the depths of the sea.
Hump of a camel, crown of a queen,
Heart of a troll, spiteful and mean.
Howl of a ghost, legs from a frog,
Oozing mud from a slimy bog.

Stir it up and make it thick,
Drink it up to make you sick.

Krystina Houghton (13)

A BAD PLACE

So many people fled
But so many were dead
They died in their beds
With maggots crawling through their heads.

The village was a ghost town
You could only hear a shiver
With the birds
Dying in the river.

Then I realised the famine was rife
It would suck all the life
From this beautiful place
There was no more race.

I was walking through the ruins
And then I found the burial ground
The bodies were rotten
They were wrapped up in cotton.

I screamed and I fled
This place was dead.

James Robertson (13)

13

Now I've turned 13,
I've realised life can sometimes be mean.
I have new ambitions and dreams,
I love designer jeans.
My room seems different because I'm keeping it clean.
It's not hard being 13.

Terri Mobbs (13)

TEENAGERS

Teenagers are known for
Greasy hair and spots,
Lots of hormonal changes,
Don't forget the strops!

Too old to throw tempers
And to get our own way,
Too young to understand,
We need to have our say!

Radios pumping,
Turned on full blast,
We never turn them off
Even when we're asked!

We are told we spend time,
Locked up in our room,
But that's because of homework
We're always in a gloom!

These long years,
Can be really rough,
If you help us through them,
They won't be so tough!

Hanisha Sethi (13)

MY FIRST CRUSH

My first real crush,
Whenever I see him I get such a rush,
I get such a warm feeling.
My heart's quickly beating,
I fall off my stool,
'Cause I can't keep my cool.

The way that he looks,
The way that I'm love struck.
He lured me into his net,
My heart is set.
Everytime I see him I want more,
I love him to his core.

He's like sweet,
That makes the lovebird's tweet.
He makes my heart sink,
My cheeks have gone pink.

In my hand I hold a rose,
The one I hold under his nose.
The bird I set free is a dove,
Maybe, maybe this is love.

Jennifer Chan (13)

JUST ONCE AGAIN

I'm down in the dumps,
Don't ask me why,
There's a good reason
I just have to cry.

What I'd give
To see your face just once more
Knowing it's impossible
Makes me run to the door.
To feel your warm, caring,
Arms surround me again
Then to look in your eyes
To know all will be well.

All I now have is memories,
I'd hate to forget
Knowing this prospect leads me to fret
Oh why can't I just
See your face once again.

Maja Kozic (15)